Nick Park
Library & Learning Centre
Tel: 01772 225304

The Three Peaks of Yorkshire

Text: Harry Rée
Photographs: Caroline Forbes

Whittet Books Ltd London

First published 1983 by Wildwood House
This edition published 1988
Text © 1983 by Harry Rée
Photographs © 1983 by Caroline Forbes
Maps © 1983 by Sue Lawes

Whittet Books Ltd, 18 Anley Road, London W14 0BY

British Library Cataloguing in Publication Data

Rée, Harry
    The Three Peaks of Yorkshire.
    1. Walking – England – Craven (North Yorkshire) –
    Guide-books   2. Craven (North Yorkshire) –
    Description and travel – Guide-books
    I. Title   II. Forbes, Caroline
    796.5′1′0942841   DA670.C88

    ISBN 0-905483-62-6

Printed and bound in Great Britain
by The Camelot Press Ltd, Southampton

Contents

The Photographs are for Tyler

Park Fell, Simon Fell and
Ingleborough

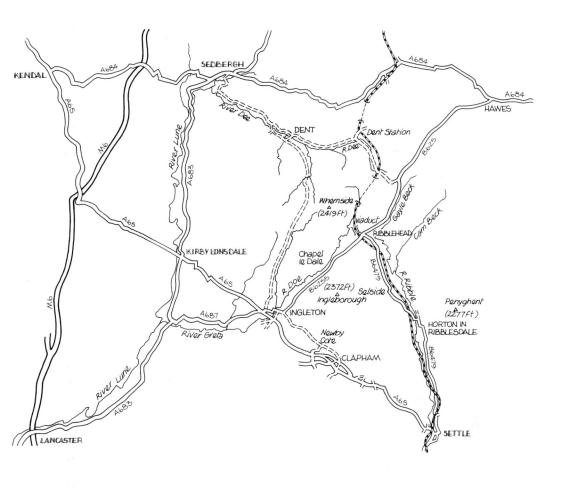

KENDAL
A684
SEDBERGH
A684
HAWES
A684
A65
M6
River Lune
River Dee
A683
DENT
Dent Station
R.Dee
B625
Whernside
(2419ft)
Viaduct
Gayle Beck
Carn Beck
RIBBLEHEAD
A65
KIRBY LONSDALE
Chapel
le Dale
B6255
R.Dee
(2372ft)
Ingleborough
B6479
Selside
R. Ribble
Penyghent
(2277ft.)
HORTON IN
RIBBLESDALE
M6
A687
INGLETON
Newby
Cote
River Greta
CLAPHAM
B6479
A65
River Lune
A683
A65
SETTLE
LANCASTER

GENERAL MAP

Key to maps

→ Heavy lines and arrows show route to be followed

→ Light arrows show alternative route or return route

········· Footpath or recommended route where there is no path

– – – Track

= = = Lane

▬▬▬ Main road (A) or (B)

▦▦▦ Railway line

River or stream

Bridge

Rock Feature

⛪ Church

■ Building

○ Pot hole or cave

🌲 Woodland

Gate

Stile

Preface

I have been having friends to stay in my house on the slopes of Ingleborough for nearly twenty years. This has meant that often I have walked with them, or suggested walks to them. I started here as a foreigner, coming from distant York. I knew nothing, before coming, of the delights and curiosities of the area but I became trapped, first by the colours and shapes, then by the air and the winds, then by the people. As each year passed I realised that I was gradually increasing my store of interesting facts and stories about my New Found Land. Walking and talking with my guests I naturally shared my newly acquired knowledge, and I began to be looked upon not so much as a mine of information, more as a rag bag. One day, talking in the pub with some genuine natives (which means people not merely born here, but having at least grandparents who were), I discovered that I knew a few things that even they didn't.

I decided then that I might convert my perambulatory conversation pieces into a book, attaching my bits of local knowledge and gossip to a series of good walks on and over the Three Peaks, Ingleborough, Penyghent and Whernside. But instead of being accompanied by familiar friends, I would take my readers along with me, mentioning odd points which would come to mind as I took them through the countryside. Such observations would be sparked off by some passing feature – an old limekiln, a curlew circling overhead and uttering its familiar piercing cry, or some peculiar rocks, an unexpected cave or a flock of foreign-looking sheep.

This explains the plan of the book. I have recommended six longish walks, all starting from a village on the edge of the area and ending at the hub, Ribblehead. Pre-Beeching there was a station there, but now only a welcome pub, built at the same time as the famous and now threatened viaduct (see page 74). The T-junction at Ribblehead is a point where many motorists and campers seem to settle down, few of them looking as

9

though they have walked very far, or intend to. But they are no doubt attracted by a grassy place to picnic, a rushing stream, the Station Inn, and by the occasional presence of a Mother Courage caravan dispensing refreshments.

However, no reader need do the whole length of any of the walks at one go. Indeed it might be stupid to try. Most of them could take five hours or more, there and back. If the whole stretch is envisaged, and two cars are available, it is a good idea to leave one car at the destination and drive to the starting point. It is of course always possible to stop on the way and go back to the start; views are often surprisingly different on the way back. I have also suggested diversions and shorter versions of the main walk, some of which return to the starting point.

Anyhow, I presume anyone reading this book can read a map, and can therefore plan their own walks, using my suggested routes as a good cook uses a recipe book, as a stimulator, and not necessarily to be exactly followed. There is in fact no need for readers to do any walking at all. Vicarious delight may surely be sought, and I hope found, merely by reading these accounts of walks enjoyed. Quite honestly my hope is that the book will give particular pleasure to those whose walking days are done, or nearly done. I certainly can increasingly sympathise with them.

The basic design is that each of three of the walks takes in the summit of one of the Three Peaks; the other three cover the area between the valley bottom and the highest contour, walking along roads or paths or tracks which hug the sides of the hills. By interrupting the walks at various points with odd bits of information, quotations or observations, I hope ultimately to have given readers something of the taste of this small area, something of its grandeur and its little details; something of its ever-changing but always appropriate colours, something of its atmosphere and spirit. This is why, in addition to the six basic walks, with their occasional diversions, I have included also, between the walks, a number of interludes in which I have gone somewhere, without saying exactly where, perhaps of an evening, perhaps very early in the morning, to savour some particular effect produced by the time of day, by the season and by the natural surroundings. My hope is that whether the book is just dipped into or conscientiously read, the Genius of the Place – the *feel* of the Three Peaks – will be passed on.

But far more evocative than anything I have written are the photographs by Caroline Forbes, who has tramped the countryside at all seasons and in all weathers, and has I think most cunningly captured that *Genius Loci*. So the writing I have done, without, except on rare occasions, being directly related to the pictures, serves, I hope, as a relevant commentary, rather than the pictures serving the writing. They stand proudly as a commentary in their own right.

One small point. Walking companions are not always attentive to a talking companion. Why should they be? Often they miss some point made by the talker. This excuses and explains occasional repetitions which occur in the text; if readers find themselves irritated and saying: 'But he's already mentioned that', I will be neither surprised nor insulted. Any reader who does notice a repetition has been more attentive than I expected.

Finally, I have to thank a large number of people, mostly local people, for their help given, sometimes unconsciously, sometimes by reading parts of my typescript and correcting errors, often by answering my incessant questions.

Many names would be included if I were to mention all who helped me, but I must especially thank the following:

David Crutchley   Author of *The Geology of the Three Peaks* (Dalesman, 1981), schoolteacher living in Clapham

Dr John Farrer   Lord of the Manor, Ingleborough Estate Office, Clapham

Alan Greenbank   Landlord of the Hill Inn, Chapel le Dale

George Horner   Signalman in the Blea Moor Box (retired)

Barbara Hutton   Chairman of the North Yorkshire Vernacular Buildings Study Group

Alan King   Community Centre Warden, Ingleton

Betsy Mason   Lodge Hall Farm, Horton in Ribblesdale

Bill Mitchell   Editor of *The Dalesman*, Clapham

Jim and Margaret Morphet   Farmers, The Shaws, Selside

Helen Sergeant   Member of Leeds University Speleological Association; Secretary, Horton Parish Council

Joe Shevelan   Warden, Yorkshire Dales National Park

Thanks too to Sue Bagshaw of Bentham who typed the manuscript, and to Edward Blishen and Jonathan Rée who corrected the typescript and made many helpful and encouraging suggestions.

Of the many authors I have quoted no name occurs more frequently than that of Arthur Raistrick and therefore to him, the greatest authority on all aspects of the Yorkshire Dales, I offer sincere thanks and respectful admiration.

This book would never have happened if Rathan Sippy of Wildwood House had not been staying with me and subsequently put the idea of it into the right heads.

Postscript from Caroline Forbes:

I would like to thank Roger Hallam and Fay Godwin who taught me how to take pictures, and thanks also to Tania George and Dmitri Kasterine.

Penyghent

Introduction to the Three Peaks

Daniel Defoe glanced this way in 1720 (or thereabouts) as he journeyed north. But he hurried on, attracted neither by the 'monstrous high hills' on his right nor by the city of Lancaster on his left. 'The town is ancient; it lies as it were in its own ruins and has little to recommend it but a decayed castle and a more decayed port. . . We were, as it were, locked in between the hills on one side, high as the clouds, and prodigiously higher, and the sea on the other, and the sea itself seemed desolate and wild. . . Nor were the hills high and formidable only, but they had an inhospitable terror in them, all barren and wild.' (Defoe: *A Tour through the Whole Island of Great Britain*)

These inhospitable wild hills certainly included the Three Peaks – Ingleborough, Whernside and Penyghent – and although for large parts of the year they are wrapped in cloud and lashed by rain, and often deserve to be called 'inhospitable', at other rarer times they are warmly friendly, lying comfortably on their valley slopes, which are, very occasionally, bathed in sunshine. Here the word Peaks, if it gives an impression of sharp-pointed Matterhorns, is wholly misleading. The Three Peaks of Yorkshire, although, like the Matterhorn, possessing unmistakable profiles, have summits which are either flat or gently rounded, and the billowing land between is, surprisingly, open and welcoming.

There are other delights; the dominant colours are greys and greens and soft browns, which gently change with the ever-changing light, while often the air, as at Macbeth's castle, 'nimbly and sweetly recommends itself'.

If Defoe had turned off to the right when he reached the city of Lancaster, as one might today turn off towards Kirkby Lonsdale at Junction 34 of the M6, he would have followed the winding Lune (giving its name both to the city and to the dale) for about ten miles and branched off right again where the Greta joins the Lune east of Cantsfield. He might then have followed the Greta up to Ingleton, which once proudly announced to motorists coming from Settle along the A65 that it is the Gateway to the Dales.

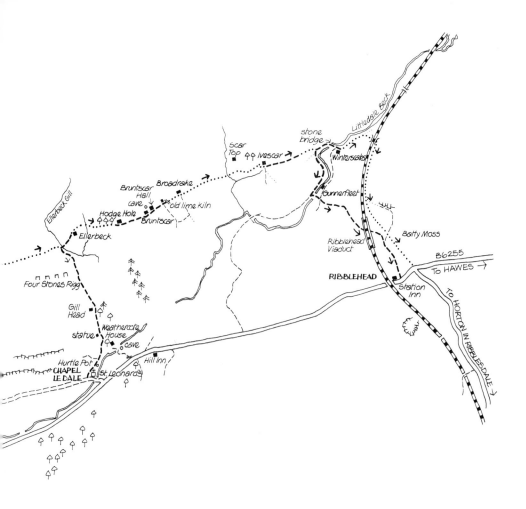

Littledale Beck

stone
bridge

Scar
Top   Ivescar
                                    Winterscales

Broadrake
Bruntscar
Hall
Cave   old lime kiln   Gunnerfleet
Hodge Hole
          Bruntscar   Batty Moss

Ellerbeck Gill
                                              Ribblehead
          Ellerbeck   Viaduct
                                                                  B6255
                                                                  To HAWES →
Four Stones Rigg
                                              RIBBLEHEAD

Gill   Station
Head   Inn
statue   Weathercote
          House
          cave   TO HORTON IN RIBBLESDALE
Hurtle Pot   Hill Inn
CHAPEL
LE DALE   St Leonard's

Ingleton Glens

Chapter 1   Ingleton to Ribblehead by the Side of Whernside

Ingleton is certainly one of the main gates to the Three Peaks, and apart from looking rather tidier today, the heart of the village probably hasn't changed much since Defoe's day. Today, as then, there is no railway station, although a hundred years ago there were two. There is no coalmine, although fifty years ago there was a flourishing one. And the impressive viaduct spanning the valley today carries no trains. So the village has a history. There used to be a large cotton mill below the church. George Armitstead from Clapham, with three partners, bought a barn there in 1791, and built a spinning mill. Was it to such people that a Mr Blakey was referring when he told Lord Torrington in 1792 that 'the Manchester Trade' was now creeping into the Dales, telling his Lordship about 'the wonderful importation of children purchased in London at so much a half score (9 sound and 1 cripple) by those merchants the most forward against the slave trade. . .' (*Torrington Diaries*; reprinted Methuen 1970). Later in his diary, Lord Torrington recounts how:

> Upon Ingleton Bridge I met a fellow, sensible I thought as speaking to my sentiments, for to my insidious enquiry 'If the cotton trade did not benefit the poor?' He answered: 'The worst thing in the world, in my opinion, Sir, for it leaves us neither stout husbandmen, nor modest girls, for the children bred in the cotton mill never get exercise nor air, and are all impudent and saucey.'

Armitstead's Mill lasted till 1854, when it was burnt down. It was rebuilt, changed hands and was again burned down in 1904. The building is now a rustic ruin. Remarkable photographs of that fire are to be found in John Bentley's *Old Ingleton* (Ingleton Publications, 1976).

There was also for many years a noisome tannery. The colliery was opened a year before the First World War, and closed a few years before the Second. Little remains of it now, except a few old slag heaps disguised by grass and trees, and near to it the New Village, built for the miners by the company. Although carefully designed and no doubt considered a model in its day, it is not an architectural masterpiece, and is fortunately not visible from the original village.

The opening of the coalmine in fact changed Ingleton in other ways, because it brought in a large number of 'foreigners' from other mining areas, such as South Yorkshire, Durham and even South Wales, so that the population is possibly less purely 'Craven' than that of other nearby villages. (The name Craven is given to a large area of north-west Yorkshire. It is thought to be derived from 'craf', a Celtic word for wild garlic, which is common in the district.)

Thomas Gray stayed at the vicarage at Chapel le Dale, and called Ingleton a 'pretty village, situated at the foot of that huge monster of nature, Ingleborough'. It is still a pretty village, with many of its grey stone houses unobtrusively colour-washed in pastel shades. There's little however to detain the sightseer except inside the much restored church of St Mary. Since it was first built, probably in the 13th century, the nave has had to be rebuilt twice, because the foundations slipped: the reason for this is simply that those who planned to put it there, on the site of a glacial moraine (i.e. rubble and gravel deposited in a long heap by a melting glacier), didn't remember the fate of those who don't build their houses on rock.

The circular 13th-century font is worth inspecting. It spent a couple of hundred years in the nearby quarry, having been thrown out by Cromwell's men, who presumably disapproved of the bas-relief sculptures around the outside. It was rescued and returned to the church, but must have been in a pretty bad state, for it was used as a whitewash pot until a local historian in 1830 suggested it ought to be restored. In spite of its chequered history, it is still an impressive example of late Norman carving. In fourteen panels formed by interlaced arches, bas-relief sculptures show scenes from the early life of the Virgin Mary. It is somewhat difficult to make out what all of them represent, but there is a useful pictorial key on the wall. There is also an oddly rare bible displayed on a lectern, in which the heading 'The Parable of the Vineyard' is printed as 'The Parable of the Vinegar'. The mistake was made in 1717.

Most visitors to Ingleton don't climb Ingleborough, but pay
their pennies and make their way up the Glens and down again.
Anyone who doesn't warm to the sight and sound of masses of
their fellows walking in convoy and snapping the waterfalls had
better choose to do this walk in the early morning or late on a
summer's evening, or perhaps in the depths of winter, when
there is lots of water and it will be free from jostling crowds.
Those who want to avoid crowds shouldn't do the waterfalls on
a public holiday. The walks, up the Doe and down the Greta
(sometimes called the Twiss), are quite demanding; it takes
about two hours to make the round trip, but the paths have been
eased. Steps, handrails and bridges may put some wilder
walkers off their stride, but for many they are welcome, and
there is a notable absence of litter. There are two reasons why a
visitor should do at least one of these walks. First because they
are rare and beautiful, and second because they are an object

lesson for anyone who wants to understand the interesting rock formations, not merely of these glens, but of the whole Three Peaks area.

The picturesque aspect of the Glens was delightfully recorded by J.S. Fletcher:

> The character and scenery along these becks is quite different to anything to be found in any other part of Yorkshire. . . The eye is continually amazed by the plenitude of waterfalls, deep black pools, vast masses of limestone rocks, richness of trees and shrubs and such a wealth of ferns and mosses as must needs give delight to the most blasé botanist. It is scarcely possible to attempt any description in words of the waterfalls, forces, and cataracts great and little which are met with in following the usual tourist route. (*A Picturesque History of Yorkshire*, 1899).

In which case it was probably best not to attempt a description, for the walk is indescribably beautiful; but

Thornton Force

Mr Fletcher does somewhat quaintly issue a worthwhile warning when he reaches Pecca Falls:

> Here the stream pours itself over several cascades and plunges into a pool of great depth. When the beck is in flood it is somewhat dangerous to approach too near to these falls, for the swirl of the water and the roar of the cascades is discomposing to the strongest minded. There is an instance quoted in the local guide books of a lady who fell into the pool at the foot of Pecca Falls and was drowned in the sight of her husband and friends, who were quite unable to afford her assistance.

Such a warning should be displayed today at the start of the walk. The death toll, especially of children, taken by these two becks is tragic. Any warning that can be given to visitors is worth while.

The Geology of the Dales

If the scenery is difficult to describe, the geology also is far from simple. But the walk offers an ideal opportunity to understand the rock formations of the Three Peaks and their unique landscape. For in the course of it, the geology is literally laid bare. As Norman Nicholson has written:

> To look at the scenery without trying to understand the rock is like listening to poetry in an unknown language. You hear the beauty, but you miss the meaning. (*Portrait of the Lakes*, Faber, 1963).

To do this walk is to pass through at least 400 million years of geological history. Four hundred million years ago, the earth's crust above which today we walk as we go up the Glens consisted, on the surface, of folded layers of ancient sedimentary rocks, identified by geologists as Silurian, Ordovician and Ingletonian. (The first two acquired their names from Welsh tribes which the Romans called the Silurii and the Ordovicii, who inhabited that part of Wales where geologists first found rocks of this age and type.) They might be compared to huge folded sheets of corrugated iron. After originally lying horizontal over the earth's surface, they were folded into wave shapes by intense heat and pressures, as mountain ranges and valleys began to be formed.

For a period lasting millions of years these irregular rock surfaces were covered by a warm sea. This sea was shallow and clear and of a constant temperature, conditions hospitable to the growth of corals. As the corals died, their hard spiky exteriors sank, along with the shells of dead sea creatures, onto the sea bed. Over the years layers of crushed coral and sea shell came to form a huge slice of limestone, which lay over those irregular 'basement' beds of older rocks named above. This massive slice, in some places over 500 feet thick, forms the base of a huge and varied rock formation, including coal measures, which is called Carboniferous, because it contains carbon: the name being given – as is often the case in geology – both to the rock itself and to the period in which it was formed. This limestone slice is hereabouts called the Great Scar Limestone, and any rocks occurring underneath it, or formed before it, such as the Ordovician, are (not illogically) called Pre-carboniferous.

After the Great Scar Limestone had been formed, a change of climate occurred; the level and content of that warm sea altered, and marine deposits of shale fell through the water onto the

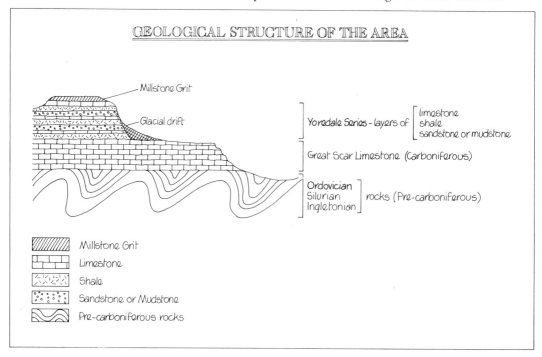

GEOLOGICAL STRUCTURE OF THE AREA

Millstone Grit

Glacial drift

Yoredale Series - layers of { limestone, shale, sandstone or mudstone }

Great Scar Limestone (Carboniferous)

Ordovician, Silurian, Ingletonian } rocks (Pre-carboniferous)

Millstone Grit
Limestone
Shale
Sandstone or Mudstone
Pre-carboniferous rocks

limestone sea bed. Then came another change, and the warm shallow seas returned. Another limestone slice was formed, but this time not so thick, for there came yet another change and deposits of shale, mud and sand landed on the limestone. Such changes occurred and recurred in sequence over millions of years, and the resultant layer-cake of rocks, composed of limestone, sandstone, shale and mudstone was named by the geologist John Phillips, in his *Geology of Yorkshire* (1836), the Yoredale (Uredale) Series. He gave it this name because that 'layer-cake' phenomenon was particularly evident on the sides of Wensleydale, previously called Yoredale after its river the Ure. Only later did the little town of Wensley, half way along the valley, claim the right of nomenclature.

However, the Yoredale Series extends well beyond Wensleydale and is laid on top of that massive block, the Great Scar Limestone, on which the Three Peaks are situated. Arthur Raistrick describes the Series graphically as:

> A rhythmic succession . . . shale followed by sandstone, sandstone followed by limestone, then shale, sandstone and limestone again. Each layer of limestone weathers out into a long scar, usually with a vertical front, and the shales weather away easily and leave the top of the limestone like the tread of a stair. The sandstones are often concealed under the scree scraped off the limestone above and form the lower part of the rise, less steep than the limestone. (*The Pennine Dales*, 1936)

Climate changes were not over yet. Topping the Yoredale Series came a deposit of grey grit and sand, which compressed into so-called millstone grit after being laid down in the delta of a huge river which once flowed over West Yorkshire from the north into the ocean. Each of our Three Peaks wears a cap of this hard and brittle sedimentary rock, which traditionally was used for millstones and whetstones, whether for grinding corn or sharpening steel.

Now comes a strange occurrence. The millstone grit itself became overlaid with swamps, where plants and great trees were able to grow. These eventually formed the coal measures, which tend to be found above millstone grit; associated with them were clays and 'red beds' consisting of a mixture of sandstones, varieties of limestone, ironstone and shale.

This geological introduction will be continued in a moment, but it is now time to return to Ingleton and to take as a starting point the confluence of the two rivers which meet under the Ingleton Viaduct. The more eastern stream starts between Gregareth and Whernside, in Kingsdale, where it is called Kingsdale Beck, but after Kingsdale it becomes the Doe. The western stream, coming from Chapel le Dale and flowing between Whernside and Ingleborough, has been called Dale Beck, the Twiss, and also the Greta. This last name has stuck and is given to the combined streams as they flow from Ingleton to join the Lune at Cantsfield. It seems that the name Greta comes from a Norse word meaning cauldron, and certainly, after heavy rains, it bubbles and froths like a boiling pot.

The Ingleton Viaduct, with its impressively tall arches, spans the Greta. It once carried trains between two local stations,

693732

Ingleton Quarry

Ingleton at the south end of the viaduct and Thornton at the northern end. They were built by two different railway companies, one operating to Carlisle in the north and starting at Thornton, the other from Skipton in the south and stopping at Ingleton. Relations between the companies at first were friendly; but the friendship did not last, and when the great Midland Railway swallowed up the little North Western, which ran from Skipton to Ingleton, the London and North Western, which owned the northern line, became a deadly rival. Such was the feeling between the two companies that passengers wishing to travel via Ingleton to or from Scotland not only had to change trains, but had to walk across the viaduct. On one occasion, Sir James Allport, the formidable general manager of the Midland, complained that his private coach from Ingleton had been conveyed north to Tebay at the back of a train of coal wagons! Today, the viaduct has no rails, and little trees and grass grow where the 'permanent' way once was; and it is closed even to pedestrians.

Under this viaduct deposits of red sandstone and large soft red rocks lie exposed on the banks of the river, and are a pointer to the coal measures beside and under Ingleton, which made the opening of the Ingleton colliery in 1913 a paying proposition. (It was closed in 1935.) But what, the curious amateur may ask, are these coal measures doing down there, when layers of millstone grit and Great Scar Limestone (which normally lie under the coal) lie hundreds of feet higher up, a little farther along the valley to the west? The explanation is the Craven Fault. This is a fracture through the layers of rock, which allowed a gigantic slippage to take place, as a result of which a huge slice of the rocky layer-cake slid down some hundreds of feet, along a fracture in the earth's crust. This explains two phenomena. First, the coal measures now under Ingleton which were once, along with the rocks on which Ingleton now stands, some hundreds of feet higher up. And secondly, the exposure, as we shall see in the Glens, of some of those old Pre-carboniferous rocks. For in some places where the slippage occurred along the fault, these older rocks were brought so close to the surface, as one block of rocks went down beside it, that when mountain streams like the Doe and the Twiss began to flow over the thin layer of limestone that at first covered them, the limestone was worn away, and these older rocks are now in places exposed.

Thornton Force, a classic
example of unconformity

It is now time to leave the viaduct and make for the car park below the church, remembering in passing that the church has twice been rebuilt in the past hundred years. Partly, as explained above, this was because it was insecurely founded on a glacial moraine, but also because of the Craven Fault, which, even over the last 1000 years, has caused the insecure foundations slightly to slip, for faulting is not a once-and-for-all event and slight slippages may occur at any time. The path leads up the right bank of the Doe, having passed under an embankment which once formed a raised single-track railway branching off the old London and North Western line near Thornton Station to collect stone from Mealbank Quarry, situated beside the parallel river, the Twiss.

The path leads gently upwards at first, through a pleasantly wooded glen where oak, ash, yew and sycamore grow randomly together on each side of the stream. This is Helk's Wood, where once Lady's Slipper orchid was said to grow in profusion until, as reported at the end of the 18th century, 'a rascally gardener of Ingleton' dug up every plant for sale (Kendal and Root: *Geology of Yorkshire*, 1924).

695746 Soon the valley narrows, the path gets steeper and a footbridge leads across to the other side of the stream. A little further on, on the right of the path, there is a rock surface marked with a kind of leprous scab, down which there may well be a trickle of water. This scabby surface is tufa, which is in fact a re-deposited limestone, formed from streams which are already saturated with lime (calcium bicarbonate). Carbon dioxide is removed from the water as it passes over vegetation, causing limestone to be re-deposited on the rocks in this rather soft, unattractive form.

694748 A little further on, the path returns to the other side via another bridge from which a spectacular view of the Pecca Falls tends to make people stop and take photographs. Here again the blue slates of Ingletonian rock rise perpendicular beside the Great Scar Limestone cliff upstream. The limestone then re-asserts itself and the landscape becomes less wooded; the path moves across pasture for a few hundred yards well above the level of the stream and then curves to the right, revealing the impressive basin into which falls the massive Thornton Force. This waterfall is nearly 50 feet high and pours over a protruding lip of Great Scar Limestone which itself rests, horizontally and 'unconformably' on a huge serrated lump of almost vertical

Ingletonian slate. (Unconformity is a geological term used to describe a situation where one type of rock lies directly on top of another, which was laid down in a quite different era.) It is fun, and usually not unsafe, to scramble over the upturned slate behind the waterfall. The line of the unconformity is easily seen. A clear horizontal indentation is stretched along the backdrop of the falls, and it is here that Arthur Raistrick, in his *Pennine Dales* (1968), vividly suggests that a hand can span between thumb and little finger worlds more than three million years apart.

697756   The path rises steeply beside the waterfall and leads on, along the stream, round a bend and over a footbridge then up a steep bank to Twisleton Lane. Some may now want to return directly to Ingleton via Beezleys, the farm at the far end of the lane and at the top of Twisleton Glen, down which the Greta (alias the Twiss) tumbles in a series of falls corresponding to, but not quite the same as, those in the Doe, not half a mile away to the west. After a right turn into Twisleton Lane a green path leads

702751   across the lower end of Scales Moor, past two farms, Scar End and Twisleton Hall; from this part of the track the ruins of the nunnery are to be seen half a mile away down the slope, looking west. The lane leads on, across a narrow road, down to

705748   Beezleys. As one walks down over the grassy slope the view of Ingleborough is possibly more impressive than from any other point. It rears up in a huge mass. Across the other side of the valley can be seen the car park and flagpole belonging to Whitescar Caves. Some may want to make for this well-visited and well-appointed attraction, and the direct route leads across the river by way of a chapelet of massive stepping stones, and so

715746   up the field and across a stile to Whitescar.

But for those intent on returning to Ingleton, there is a well-trodden path with convenient steps leading down the glen. Compared with the Doe, the Twiss has cut deeply into the rock, seeming to make use of the perpendicular slate formations which lie exposed through the limestone to dig deep narrow channels. The trees here are more uniform, mostly oak, and well spaced; the path, with frequent concrete steps, goes down

706746   steeply until, after crossing to the north by a footbridge, it reaches an old slate quarry (Ingletonian slate), and from here the path is less steep. Another disused quarry on the left: and then,

698736   across the further side, the cliff face of Mealbank Quarry, also disused, comes into view, with the seams of limestone bending downwards in a great arc, as if to make a final point in the illustrated lecture in geology to which the walker has, if willing, been subjected. For here is the solid rocky evidence of the Craven Fault, frozen for all to see.

For those who don't want to return directly to Ingleton, there are two possible choices on reaching Twisleton Lane: to turn left down the lane towards Kingsdale, or right towards Beezleys, when another route – this time leading to Ribblehead – may be taken. First the Kingsdale option.

Kingsdale lies between Whernside and Gregareth and it is worth a little attention. Looking up the dale, which stretches almost for four miles up to Kingsdale Head, it is striking how very flat is the surface, and how the line of the beck, for the first two miles from the bridge, stretches almost as straight as a Roman road, for there is little variation in the level of the ground on either side, while the incline down the valley is minimal. All this suggests that at one time, probably at the end of the final retreat of the ice which covered the area in successive stages from 500,000 to 20,000 years ago, a large lake, as long as Kingsdale, existed here. It was a lake formed by the last glacier, which, at the lower end of the dale, had deposited a huge dam of silt and mud and grit that for a time held back the water. But the waters gradually increased and, not being able to escape over the middle of the dam, found a slight indentation on the south side and began to pour over this lip. This is how the valley of the Doe began below Kingsdale, and how the river flowing over Thornton Force formed the glen described above.

710797

There are other reasons for lingering for a moment on the subject of Kingsdale. It was once called Vikingsdale, for as the name of the farm at the top, Braida Garth, suggests, it was once occupied by Viking invaders who had sailed over from the east coast of Ireland and settled there.

705776

Another reason is the fascinating and accessible Yordas Cave. It lies about three miles up the dale on the left of the road tucked away in a clump of trees. Anyone intending to explore the cave (and it is well worth exploring) should wear wellingtons, have at least one torch, and get permission from Braida Garth Farm, reached by a bridge across the beck about a mile before the cave.

705792

A number of stories are told about this cave. William Howitt, in *Rural Life of England* (1838), writes of it as 'Yorda's Cave', explaining that it is the cave of Yorda, the Danish sorceress. Another legend is recalled by Wainwright in his indispensable *Walks in Limestone Country*. He writes of Yordas, a Nordic giant who used to live in the cave and enjoyed a diet of small boys. John Housman, who is quoted extensively below, wrote at the beginning of the last century: 'Half a century ago, a lunatic escaped from his friends in Ingleton, and lived here for a week in the winter season. . . Since then a poor woman, big with child, travelling alone in this inhospitable vale to Dent, was taken in labour, and found dead in this cave.'

To describe the cave itself, no one could rival John Housman:

The cave does not appear till we get through some sheepfolds and are within a few yards of its entrance, which is rather alarming; for we no sooner descend gently through a rude arched opening, four yards by seven, like the gateway of some ancient castle, than we see stones of enormous weight pendent from the roof, apparently loose and ready to fall down upon our heads.

From these surprising objects our attention is directed to the solemn and gloomy mansions which we now enter, when the noise of a waterfall is heard at a distance. The roof rises to a height concealed in darkness; this and the slipperiness of the stones under our feet, rouses our apprehension for personal safety, and we stop short. Our guide now places himself upon a fragment of rock and strikes up his lights, consisting of six or eight candles, put into as many holes of a stick. . .

ngleton Quarry

Though under the conduct of such an experienced leader, and assured that the danger is merely imaginary, we journey on with cautious steps. On turning right we immediately lose sight of day; the noise of the cataract increases and we soon find ourselves on the brink of some subterraneous rivulet.

No cave in romance, no den of lions, giants or serpents, nor any haunts of ghosts or fairies, were ever described more frightfully gloomy and dismal than this now before us. After passing the brook and cautiously proceeding thirty or forty yards further, we are under the necessity of climbing over a rugged heap of huge rocks, which had, some time or other, fallen from the roof or sides of the cave; but now are encrusted with a smooth calcarious substance. . . On the right we observed, among several curiously encrusted figures a projecting stone which our guide called the Bishop's Throne, from its great resemblance to that appendage of a cathedral. . . Another confused mass of encrusted matter bears some resemblance to a large organ. . . We now enter a narrow pass of five or six yards, where the roof is supported by seven pillars; there is only room for one person in breadth, but the height is very considerable. We soon reached the cascade which we had heard for some time at a distance; it issues from an opening in the rock, and falls about four or five yards into a circular apartment roofed with a fine dome. This apartment some visitants have named the Chapter House. The broad sheet of water, the spray arising from the fall, and the beautiful petrifactions, all illuminated with the light of candles, produce effects in this natural edifice which the puny efforts of art may attempt to imitate, but in vain. Near the Chapter House there is an opening through which a person may creep and arrive at other large apartments; but we did not attempt the experiment. . .

We leave the dark excavations with redoubled sentiments of gratitude towards the Almighty, for the blessings he affords us in the light of the sun, which, after being buried for some time in these murky regions, we now enjoy with still greater pleasure. (John Housman: *A Descriptive Tour and Guide to the Lakes, Caves, Mountains and other Natural Curiosities in Cumberland, Westmoreland, Lancashire and parts of The West Riding of Yorkshire*, printed by F. Jollie, Carlisle, and sold by C. Law, Ave-Maria Lane, London, 1802).

One more curiosity is worth noting before leaving the subject of Kingsdale; this was described by the Rev. John Hutton, in his *Tour to the Caves*, 1781. They were being led by a curate whose services they had procured in Ingleton:

> We shaped our course along the road leading to the village of Dent. As we proceeded the curate entertained us with an account of some singular properties observable in the black earth which composes the soil in the higher parts of the vale, in various morassy places. It is a kind of *igneum lutum* or rather a sort of putrefied earth, which in the night resembles fire, when it is agitated or being trod upon. The effects it produces in a dark evening are truly curious and amazing. Strangers are always surprised, and often frightened, to see their own and horses legs being sprinkled to all appearance with fire, and sparks of it flying in every direction, as if struck out of the ground from under their feet.

In 1781 Dalton hadn't investigated marsh gas and its origins.

slabs of millstone grit

Instead of turning left in Twisleton Lane and making for Kingsdale one can go right, and then just after an iron kissing gate, a green path leads off to the left, back up the hill. Take this path. It leads round the 'bows' of Scales Moor, called Twisleton Scar End and, swinging round to the right, a wall enticingly offers the traveller a National Park step–ladder stile, to help cross the wall without dislodging any stone. This of course indicates an established right of way. However, *do not cross this stile*. It leads back down to Kingsdale Beck via Braida Garth.

Keep to the green path, which will lead up and round and over the shoulder of Twisleton Scar End, and swing north-east (or to the left). It now takes the walker over a plateau on the 1250' contour to remain at about this height for two miles or more. The sometimes grassy, sometimes stony track called Kirby Gate makes pleasant walking. ('Gate' here means 'street' or 'way' cf. Swedish: *gata*, a path; also the street names of York and elsewhere – Micklegate, Stonegate, etc.) Over the first half mile there are cairns to the right and left of the track to guide uncertain or untrusting visitors and no doubt useful in snow. Rising slightly, the path becomes peaty under foot, and the occasional pool of clean brown water indicates not only peat on top, but millstone grit underneath. Soon the limestone emerges again, and the path crosses or finds a way through extensive 'pavements'. These pavements are a feature of this limestone country, being bare 'fields' of pale grey rock, into which cracks of varying depth, length and width have been cut through the action of rainwater. The cracks are called grykes. The blocks of limestone between the grykes are called clints. Once the surface of these pavements was a flat plane, but rainwater first formed little gulleys and then, eroding the limestone, gradually turned the gulleys into often deep fissures (see page 137).

In this area huge limestone boulders can be seen perched on the top of clints, the boulders having been deposited there as the last glacier melted (only 10,000 years ago). The more distant boulders proudly show their well-shaped profiles against the skyline, and to the south a new and unfamiliar profile of Ingleborough comes into view as one draws level with the summit. It seems almost as though that 'huge monster of nature' was trying to look like Penyghent, like a huge tiger *couchant*, preparing to leap into the Lancashire plain.

What was this Kirby Gate used for? Possibly it was the twin of the Turbary Road, which runs parallel to it along the ridge of

700754

698756

700756

Gregareth, a couple of miles or so to the north with Kingsdale in between. For *Turba*ry suggests peat, deriving from the German *torf*, which means sod or peat, while the Old High German gets even closer, with *zurba*. Thus just as the Turbary Road served peat cutters, moving with their carts or sledges along the side of Gregareth, so Kirby Gate probably also served the same purpose. The big difference between the two tracks is that Turbary offers the walker today a whole series of potholes and caves, such as Rowton and Jingling Pot, and Yordas Cave, which – as indicated above – is certainly worth a visit.

But we should get back to the 1250′ contour and Kirby Gate. In its later stages, where the path is peaty, there are no potholes or caves, but a succession of swallow holes (looking like bomb craters, but in fact the beginning of putative potholes). The very last of these, on the left of the path, has been most beautifully sculptured (by rainwater of course) over thousands of years to form a vast white stone funnel with regular vertical ribs, which encloses ever narrowing gutters.

The path now becomes less and less distinct and there are no cairns, but it is still marked as a path on the map. There are two landmarks to be seen at this point. Ahead is a ruined building which turns out to be no more than a sheepfold; and off to the right, against the side of Ingleborough, the white gable-end of a house stands out. The sheepfold is interesting because of the stones of which it is built, half of them light grey limestone, angular and sharp edged, half of them of mudstone, brown and rounded. This shows that we are standing where, just under the turf, a layer of limestone is covered by a layer of mudstone. The latter is formed from the silt brought down by those fast-flowing rivers from the north, the limestone originating in those corals and shells of sea creatures living and dying in the warm still waters of the tropical lagoons which once flooded this landscape.

At this point the proper path appears again. Straight ahead is an impressive 'field' of limestone pavement, with a huge boulder of limestone perched daintily on three toes and resting on the flat base of the large clint. Turning northwards and skirting the pavement, the grassy path of Kirby Gate leads gently down to Ellerbeck Gill and a cart track. Before the beginning of the track, and over to the right, four clusters of large limestone boulders stand out white against the dark reedy grass, giving their name to the ridge – Four Stones Rigg. They are not of great interest, but two of them have that strange 'capping' of white limestone, a kind of protective tam o' shanter hat, which looks as though it had been sloshed on while the mix was still soft, and had dropped a little drunkenly down the side of the rock.

731783

Such thoughts are enough to turn attention to that aforementioned gable-end, because from here field glasses are hardly needed to pick out a three letter word, spelt out in black letters against the white wall: INN! This is the Hill Inn standing beside the Ingleton–Hawes Road, where it has been for over three hundred years. It's one of the best pubs in the area, many would say the best. The thought of that generously long, curved bar, the bare wooden planks of the floor and the exposed beams, some of them resting on the grey stone walls, the little, unspoilt Britannia tables, the roaring fire, and above all the Theakston's beer, may well cause travellers to divert; having reached Ellerbeck Gill, they will go neither to the left, to look where the water pours out of a modest limestone scar, nor straight over the ford on through Ellerbeck Farm, but will carry on down the tracks towards the recently planted tree breaks, past Gillhead, a whitewashed house with a flagpole, and down the respectably tarmacadamed lane to Chapel le Dale and the pub. In spring (and this may well be the month of May up here at 1,000 feet) the sides of the lane are enlivened by clusters of daffodils and a variety of conifers and budding rowan trees, while halfway down on the right is a pleasant shock, a welded bronze statue, about six foot tall, of a warrior, who seems to be challenging with bow and arrow anyone coming up, for this is a bridle path, with a right of way only for walkers or horse riders.

The sculpture is the work of a former teacher at the College of Trinity and All Saints, Leeds, Charles I'Anson, and was placed there by the owner of the end house on this track, Gillhead. It is he who has been responsible for planting many trees and bulbs on each side of this track and he surely deserves gratitude.

Other surprises lie in store before the bottom is reached. Hurtle Pot lies to the left of the track. It is deep and dark and overhung with trees. A boggart (a wicked fairy in Yorkshire folk lore) is supposed to haunt it and lure people into the pool seventy feet down, where black trout are said to be lurking!

738773   After this, the Church of St Leonard at Chapel le Dale is worth a visit. It is the Chapel of Ease served by the vicar of Ingleton. (A Chapel of Ease eased the journey of those who found the long walk to the parish church of a Sunday rather too much.) Small, with a low roof, it contains a marble tablet on the left of the entrance 'to the memory of those who through accident lost their lives in constructing the railway works between Settle and Dent Head'. It further mentions that the tablet was provided by 'their fellow workmen and the Midland Railway Company'. The Company also paid to buy land for the extension of the cemetery, but whether it was big enough to contain the hundred or so workmen who died of disease or accident while constructing the railway works is very doubtful. The original church cemetery was described by Robert Southey in his novel *The Doctor*:

> The turf was as soft and fine as that of the adjoining hills; it was seldom broken, so scanty was the population to which it was appropriated . . . and the few tombstones which had been placed there were themselves half buried. The sheep came over the wall where they listed, and sometimes took shelter in the porch from the storm. Their voices and the cry of the kite wheeling above were the only sounds which were heard there except when the single bell tinkled for service on the Sabbath day, or with a slower tongue gave notice that one of the children of the soil was returning to the earth from which he sprung.

The road from the church leads down over a low bridge, under which Dale Beck (alias the Twiss or Greta) seldom flows: that is, the water from Whernside normally disappears underground at this point, leaving the stony river bed quite dry; but occasionally storms are so sudden and heavy that water swirls down over the rocks and at such times the bridge is not high enough to take all the water underneath it, but gaps in the parapet allow the flood waters to flow temporarily over as well as under it. Shortly after the bridge the road joins the old turnpike road from Ingleton to Hawes. Up the hill to the left lies the pub, but almost immediately on the left of the road a private drive leads to Weathercote. The house was visited by Walter White on his tour in 1770, and although Victorian additions have been made, his description of it holds good two centuries later: 'Standing on a sheltered valley slope, with a flower garden in front and trees around, the house presents a favourable specimen of a yeoman's residence.' Weathercote cave is behind the house, and in the past was much visited by the eminent. A water-colour painting of it by Turner done in 1808 or 1809 is in the Graves Art Gallery, Sheffield (No 2279), and another in the British Museum, this one done in 1817-18. Both pictures are reproduced in Andrew Wilton's *The Life and Work of J.M.W. Turner*, Academy Editions, 1979. As the cave is on private land, it can be visited only with special permission, and therefore descriptions of it, from two separate observers, follow:

First, the Rev. John Hutton in his *Tour to the Caves* (1781):

> We came to Weathercote Cave, the most surprising curiosity of the kind in the island of Great Britain. It is a stupendous subterranean cataract in a huge cave, the top of which is on the same level as the adjoining lands. On our approach, our

A party of cavers with Whernside in the background

ears and eyes were equally astonished with the sublime and terrible. The cave is of a lozenge form and divided into two by a rugged and grotesque arch of limestone rock. . . Having descended with caution from rock to rock, we passed under the arch and came into the great cave, where we stood some time in silent astonishment to view this amazing cascade . . . near eleven yards from the top issues a torrent of water out of a hole in the rock, about the dimensions of a large door in a church, sufficient to turn several mills . . . it falls twenty-five yards at a single stroke on the rocks at the bottom, with a noise that amazes the most intrepid ear. The water sinks as it falls amongst the rocks at the bottom, running by a subterranean passage about a mile, where it appears again by the side of the turnpike road. . . The cave is filled with spray and the sun happening to shine very bright, we had a small vivid rainbow within a few yards of us, for colour, size and situation, perhaps nowhere else to be equalled. A huge rock that had sometime been rolled down by the impetuosity of the stream, and was suspended between us and the top of the cascade, like the coffin of Mahomed at Medina, had an excellent effect in the scene. . . We were tempted to descend into a dark chamber at the very bottom of the cave . . . and from thence behind the cascade, at the expense of having our clothes a little wet and dirtied.

The Rev. John Hutton resisted that temptation, but Walter White, in his *Month in Yorkshire* (1858), had been more daring:

To descend lower seems scarcely possible, but you do get down, scrambling over the big stones to the very bottom, into the swirling shower of spray. Here a deep recess or chamber at one side affords good standing ground . . . conversation is difficult, for the roar is overpowering. After I had stood for some minutes, Mr Metcalf [the name of the owner of the house, who was acting as guide] told me that it was possible to get behind the fall and look through it . . . I buttoned my overcoat to my chin and rushed into the cavity . . . I was in a pit 120 feet deep, covered by a tumultuous curtain of water, but had to make a speedy retreat, so furiously was I enveloped in blinding spray. To make observations from that spot one should wear a suit of waterproof.

How right he was!

The diversion above, at Ellerbeck Gill, with suggestion of a visit to the Hill Inn, may of course not have been so tempting for everyone. Although Kirby Gate ends at Ellerbeck Gill, it is well worth continuing straight on towards the great Ribblehead Viaduct a couple of miles ahead. The path now becomes a bridle way and, apart from tractors and cars having business with the farms strung out along the northern side of the track, stray motorists are, not unnaturally, unwelcome. This makes it all the pleasanter for walking. The names of the farms give a clear hint as to their ethnic origins – no Latin influence here. After Ellerbeck comes Bruntscar Hall, then Bruntscar Farm, and after that Broadrake, Ivescar, Gunnerfleet and Winterscales. The track twists through the Ellerbeck farmyard. The buildings themselves are old, but the house has lost its original roof of heavy local slates, which have been replaced by corrugated cement rectangles, not very pretty but better than galvanised corrugated iron for they weather well to match the grey uneven limestone of the walls. Shortly after the farm a wood of mature sycamores lines the road on the left, and the impressive natural wall of huge limestone rocks has given hospitality to quite large mountain ash trees, which have squeezed themselves outwards and upwards from between the cracks in the cliff face. The man-made wall which occasionally runs along the top of the cliff wall is peculiar because it's a 'single' – that is, only one stone thick – and the light from the sky behind it is strangely filtered, as through an irregularly wide-meshed sieve. At the end of the wood, on the left of the road, is an old 'laithe' or barn which one might pass by without noticing. This would be a mistake. It is marked as Hodge Hole on the os map, but there is no trace of a pot hole nearby. It may once have been called Hodge's Hall, more likely than not as a joke against 'Hodge' – the traditional name for a farmer's boy – who lodged there, for it was obviously built not only as a barn for storage, but as a place for someone (perhaps Hodge) to live in. At the eastern end of the building there is a diminutive section which contains an interior stone stairway leading to a first floor room (the floor being somewhat flimsy and dangerous now) containing a large lintelled fireplace, directly above a similar fireplace in the room below. There is no chimney, nor any sign of one. In the storage section of the barn one wall shows a blocked up opening which would allow a cart to get in, but it is only eight feet high. The roof consists of the original thick local slates, and is carried on very rough beams, one of which does not disguise its origin, for it forks at the end into two thick branches.

737788

The next house along the track is Bruntscar Farm, a long white building, newly re-furbished. It is succeeded almost immediately by Bruntscar Hall. This consists of two houses joined, the western end unfortunately crumbling, although the roof still holds. The kitchen contains a wide fireplace with a beehive oven, and the lintel of the inhabited house is a stone dated 1689. Behind the house, unexpectedly, is Bruntscar Cave. It leads straight into Whernside for about 500 yards, but anyone exploring it needs a torch, rubber boots, something, preferably a caver's helmet, to protect the head from bumps on the roof, and (most important) permission to go in from the householder, for it is on his land. After leaving Bruntscar, the track continues for about 200 yards in the same direction, passing a limekiln, tactically placed as usual (see page 64) to facilitate cartage of lime

Limestone pavements

Ribblehead Viaduct looking east

and fuel. After this the track leads up towards the slopes of Whernside, but this is a trick, except for someone who really wants to climb up Whernside by the least interesting route. Immediately ahead a little gate into a field opens on to a footpath, which is the Right of Way to the next farm, Broadrakes. Passing in front of the farm buildings the path continues on the level, over a stream (Scar Top Gill) which is often dried up, but which, after rain, is fed from a high waterfall which sweeps over the edge of the scar. Further along on the left is a strangely inappropriate modern timber house, looking rather Swedish, but even in this landscape out of place. Then comes Ivescar; the path leads through the yard and joins once more a cart track to reach Winterscales. A beautiful small stone bridge leads across to Winterscales farm itself, a traditional stone house with a strange and awkward addition on the southern end – a large thirties bungalow with a roof of wooden shingles instead of slates. The often muddy path leads through the yard beside Littledale Beck and towards the railway; it passes under a bridge and joins the path down to Batty Moss and the great Ribblehead Viaduct with its twenty-four arches. An alternative route to Ribblehead branches off to the right just before the bridge at Winterscales, onto a macadamed road which winds down past Gunnerfleet and leads under the viaduct itself. The road leads across lumpy ground which once supported the shanty town of Sebastapol, one of the five between the viaduct and Blea Moor tunnel. One of these was called Belgravia (reserved for the managers), the others being Jerusalem, Jericho and Salt Lake. The latter is the only shanty-town whose name has stuck, to be preserved on the os map. For in 1870 the Midland Railway built a line of six very urban-looking cottages beside the Salt Lake quarry for their linesmen and signalmen. Some of the cottages are still lived in by retired railwaymen. Why Salt Lake? Supposedly a group of the railway navvies had previously worked laying the track of the Union Pacific. One final tip. If the walk is planned to finish at the viaduct on a sunny afternoon in autumn or winter, the setting sun on the viaduct, as you approach it, lights a dramatic scene, and the shadow you throw, as you walk between the arches, makes you seem twenty feet tall – and so the viaduct is only five times your height!

738791

754802

759795

Cold Spring Morning

The tops were mist-covered this morning but I decided to walk.
I drove to where an old track led up from the road through
some long-disused mine workings and then died out. Branching
off across some short turf to a high wall ahead, I found
'throughs' to step on (see page 187) climbed up, jumped off and
landed on the edge of a little landscape of limestone pavements.
I leapt from clint to clint, as if crossing a broken-up arctic
icefield. A beautifully made wall enclosed the pavements, but
there was a convenient gap. From there a sheep track led up
steeply through a corridor bounded by irregular white rocks or
rather small cliffs, with long, wrinkled faces like the later
Auden.

I pushed on upwards between these fluted blocks of limestone
and arrived on a plateau of pavements which gleamed white and
wet. To the east the sun suddenly appeared through the mist,
and away ahead the massive mountainside showed itself –
sideface to its best advantage. The ground started sloping
downhill and in front I could see hundreds of small brown
boulders perched on the white limestone, a scatter of little
islands in that Sargasso Sea of browny green grass. A wisp of
mist came at me and I went through it to inspect one of the
boulders; it jumped up and ran off to join a group of other sheep
grazing beyond the rocks! But not all those rocks were sheep;
they were erratics, carried from further up the hill by the last of
the glaciers and deposited ten thousand years ago on this, their
alien bed. Unexpectedly the limestone pavement came to an
end, succeeded by rough tufted grass and soft boggy soil, where
shallow pools were lined with shiny dark green moss growing
beside and under the water.

I came on a deep crater, followed by two more in a line as if a stick of bombs had been released over the mountain by a damaged plane in the war. In the deepest crater a sheep was nosing around the cave entrance forty feet below. I must have disturbed it, as it leapt like a gazelle up the side to join its friends.

I walked on over peaty moss and joined the 'recommended' path up the mountain. The popularity of the path was confirmed by orange peel and coke tins among the stones as well as by the patterned prints of many bootsoles in the frozen mud. No one but me was walking it today; it is dark brown and pebbly – still frozen over but with a *crème brulé* surface, which allowed my boots to crackle through. I sank hardly at all into the frozen mud and peat. Tiny streams ran down the ruts in the path, and in places big fat tadpoles seemed to be pushing their way continually down under the glass cover of the ice – air bubbles of course.

For a second the mist blew away down the side of the mountain and I could see the cairn at the top, and then it was wrapped up again. Panting as I reached it, I climbed up on it. The wind in the stones made an Aeolian note – it occurred to me I was standing on a stone instrument and I was wrapped around in mist. I haven't felt so alone for years.

Drumlins in Ribblesdale

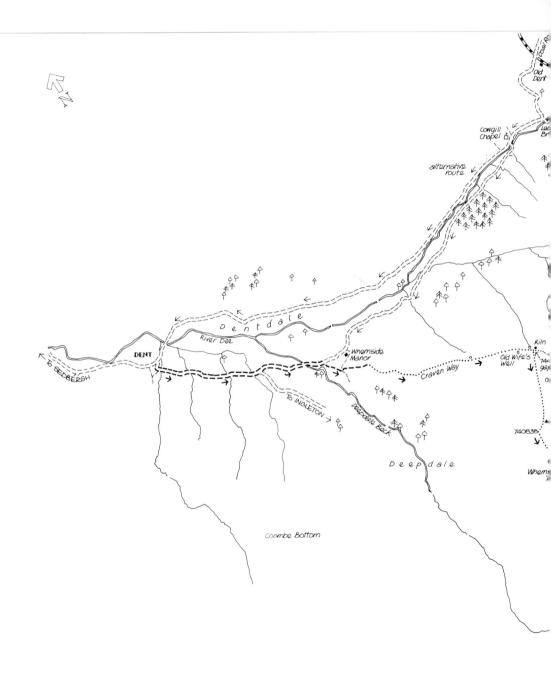

N

To Dent R
Old
Dent

Cowgill
Chapel

Lea
Br

alternative
route

Dentdale

River Dee

Kiln

DENT

Whernside
Manor

Old Wife's
Well

74
98/

Craven Way

To SEDBERGH

To INGLETON

Deepdale Beck

740838

Deepdale

Wherns

Coombe Bottom

Dent
Fell

To HAWES

B6255

Stonehouse
Farm

Artangill
Viaduct

barn

tsman
Inn

River Dee

Dent
Youth
Hostel

Dent Head
Viaduct

alternative path
to Ribblehead

Tunnel (2622 yds)

Blea Moor

Force Gill

Knoutberry Hill

junction
of walls

waterfall

Coal Gill

aqueduct

Greensett
Tarn

route by road
to Dent

B6255

nernside
ummit
419 ft)

Little Dale Beck

B6479   To HORTON IN RIBBLESDALE

RIBBLEHEAD

Ribblehead
Viaduct

Station
Inn

route by road
to Dent via
Ingleton and
Kingsdale

Peat Bog on Whernside

Chapter 2 From Dent up Whernside and down to Ribblehead

It may be the tallest of the Three Peaks, reaching 2419 feet, but for many people it is the least attractive either to climb or to look at. (One unwitting young walker thought it was called Wormside.) But it's only fair to admit that it can be dazzlingly beautiful in the early morning sun, with a sprinkling of snow decorating the ridge and a pale blue sky behind. Some enthusiasts try and bag it quickly, rushing up it from the viaduct and down again the same way. But doing this has led some panting climbers to ask themselves why they 'do' mountains at all. There are at least two better routes to the top, and they can be combined into one long walk. Better still, perhaps, the unambitious can enjoy the walk without ever having to drag themselves up the last rather boring 500 feet to the top, which involves tramping over a mile or more of tussocky reeds and bogs. But only the strong-willed and sophisticated, or the very weary of course, can resist the magnetic pull of the trig point on this highest of the Three Peaks; and if it's a fine clear day the magnetism should not be resisted. The view from the top is superb through 360 degrees.

Before starting to climb it, let's get the name sorted out. The fact that local farmers are said to have used the sand from the Whernside Tarns for sharpening their scythes, that the gritstone from the capping of the mountain made much valued whetstones, and that one of the other names for gritstone is *millstone* grit; all these match the supposition that the rock from the higher reaches of Whernside was used for making *querns*. (Small handmills for grinding corn or pepper. Examples of them can be seen in the Pig Yard Museum and in the North Craven Museum at Settle.)

We cannot doubt, then, the suggestion of the geologist Phillips that the name was once Quernside. Besides, the name also occurs in a manuscript of the Coucher Book of Furness Abbey, where an entry dated 1203/04 refers to three vaccaries (Old English for cow pastures), Quernsyde, Souterskales and Burbaldthwaite. The first is obviously today's Whernside, the second Southerscales, but Burbaldthwaite seems to exist no more.

The most attractive composite route for 'doing' Whernside can of course be followed in either direction. For those feeling energetic it can lead right to the summit, or be looked upon as a long but pleasant afternoon's walk over the north-east shoulder of the hill, avoiding the drag to the top. The path to follow is called Cravens Way and was once used as a packhorse path from Dent to Ribblehead. It is easily the most direct route, but whether it was over a Roman road is doubtful. Jacquetta Hawkes (1954) writes cautiously that it 'is said to be one of the roads used by the Roman conquerors'. And she goes on: 'For the energetic and leisurely . . . it is well worth tracing its course, which on the high moorland is said to show as a heavily cambered and kerbed road, 20 feet wide with flagged culverts, some of which still carry water.' Those pieces of literally hard evidence are not easy to discover, but she is right in saying that it is worth tracing its course, whether Roman or not.

Most people would want to avoid doing the walk twice, that is there and back on the same day, so walkers can either be met at the end of their walk by a willing driver (and a good rendezvous point is the Station Inn at Ribblehead), or – if there's more than one with a car – it can be made into a two-car operation, leaving a car at each end of the route and, after the walk, driving to collect the second car which has been abandoned at the start. This use of a car has the advantage of a spectacular drive to or from the village of Dent via the valley of the Dee.

To get there by car from Ribblehead it is best to take the Hawes road for about 4 miles and then branch off north, where the signpost indicates Dent and Sedbergh. After less than a mile the Dent Head Viaduct comes into view. It is particularly impressive, for although it is only half as long as the one at Ribblehead, it is built across a narrow gorge and seems higher. After the viaduct, the road goes down to meet the river Dee, which flows fast over great flat slabs of dark limestone and continues beside the road for a mile or two.

Soon, on the far side of the river, and reached by a footbridge, there is a pleasant domestic-looking house which is the Dent Youth Hostel, and after about another mile, a good pub, the Sportsman's. Fortunately (but possibly not for the landlord), there will never be parking space there for more than a few cars, so it is almost never overcrowded. But before reaching the pub, the road crosses the stream. Here a short diversion on foot is strongly recommended. Leave the car just before reaching the bridge and take the track up from the bridge past Stone House Farm. This is the home ground of the so-called Dent Marble. Two marble mills once operated here, powered by the waters of Arten Gill, which flows fast over rocks beside the track into the Dee. They turned machinery for cutting and polishing the hard limestone which was quarried nearby. The marble effect, which shows up when polished, is given by the fossils of coral or sea lily (crinoids) embedded in the stone. Between the tracks and

772858

the stream, just after the farm, a tall two-storey barn with glassless windows stands on its own. This was the lower mill and once contained the great iron water wheel, 60 feet in diameter, referred to by Arthur Raistrick (*The Dalesman*, 1952). In relating the story of Dent Marble he unearthed another story about William Armstrong, founder of the famous Armstrong's Factory in Newcastle who, when he was an articled clerk in a lawyer's office in Newcastle, came on holiday here in 1835. Walking up Arten Gill past the mills, he worked out that the water power was being most inefficiently used. His interest grew and when he returned home to Newcastle he had a rotary hydraulic machine made. It worked; so he abandoned the law and became one of the great industrial kings of the North East. His factory has entered the Geordie folk song repertoire, as they stream past it 'Gangin' along the Scotswood Road/To see the Blaydon Races'.

The track continues up beside the gill. It is an old packhorse road from Dent over Dent Fell to Widdale Bridge on the road to Hawes. Today it is stony and steep, enclosed for the first mile or two by limestone walls. Directly ahead is the famous Arten Gill Viaduct, built of Dent Marble (unpolished of course). If the afternoon sun strikes it, the great stones of the huge piers take on a greenish brown tinge – very impressive against a blue sky. The viaduct has eleven arches; two of the highest span the gill and are more than twice the height of the ones at each end. Above the middle arch, high up on the wall which runs along the top, the date **1875** stands out proudly, carved clearly in the stone.

The whole structure seems more solid and clean than the great Batty Moss Viaduct with its 24 arches at Ribblehead. Passing underneath and looking up from the track one can see that the semi-circular underside of each arch is clean and smooth, the trimmed stones as closely joined together as they were 100 years ago; no need here for the brick lining which had been necessary at Ribblehead. Sadly however, as at Ribblehead, this magnificent structure is giving trouble. After a few consecutive days and nights of hard frost, train drivers have to slow down to 5 mph as they cross it because (as I was told by one of them who had been working that line for 33 years) over every pier, after such a frost, the line rises with the ballast nearly a foot as the water, which now seeps through and down into the rubble inside the piers, freezes and expands. 'It's like going over a switchback,' he said.

It's worth walking up the slope beside the smaller arches to get level with the line. The huge piers are 15 feet thick at the bottom, tapering to 6 feet at the top. The foundations evidently went down 50 feet into the marshy soil.

Along the line, Dent Station is just visible to the north as the line sweeps round, smoothly stretching out across the hillside, utterly undeterred by natural hazards. What a contrast with the packhorse road which staggers from side to side up the gill, held together on each side by its now crumbling walls. The Roman road-builders must have felt a real pride in their straight-as-an-arrow roads, disdaining hills and valleys. Did the railway navvies take the same delight in their impressive single-minded conquests? The huge spoil-heaps at the southern end of the viaduct, now respectably grassed over, must have represented months of hard labour as the men dug the deep cutting which the line goes through before reaching Arten Gill; it was dug with spades and moved in wheel barrows or, if the men were lucky, in farm carts. It's worth walking over the heaps on the way back to the road, and contemplating and honouring the forgotten, not-so-eminent Victorians who worked here. For evidently the reputation of the English railway navvy spread worldwide. They were recruited to work in Canada, the States, South America and the Continent. Joseph Locke, an engineer supervising work on the Paris-Rouen line, reported that their reputation spread all over Normandy,

> where they entertained the curious Frenchmen by their dress, their manners and their uncouth size. They were generally used on the most difficult and dangerous work. They scorned the wooden shovels and basket-sized barrows which the French peasants brought to work, and used picks and shovels which only the most robust could wield. To watch them work became a new entertainment. 'Often,' said Locke, 'have I heard the exclamation of French loungers around a group of navvies: *Mon Dieu, ces Anglais, comme ils travaillent!*' (Terry Coleman: *The Railway Navvies*, Hutchinson, 1965)

The road leads pleasantly along under trees to Lea Yeat Bridge, where the old Coal Road to the Garsdale pits (disused) mounts steeply to what can now only be described as the disused railway station at Dent. The main road passes over Cowgill Beck and beside Cowgill Chapel (of which more below). After the chapel the road forks and two alternative routes lead to the village, one on the north and the other on the south side of the long and fertile valley of Dentdale. There is, it's only fair to mention, an alternative route to Dent from Ribblehead, via Ingleton and Kingsdale (see page 32). This is almost as impressive as the viaduct road beside the Dee, especially if there is snow about because the road rises to 1530 feet and includes a gradient down into Dent of 1 in 4. (Perhaps it would be worth finding out if the snow plough has been along it before trying it in the snow.)

Dent itself was once a flourishing little town. Because Dentdale is sheltered from the north, south and east by hills, the milder airstream from the west determines the climate in the valley. This explains why, in the past, cornfields and orchards were a feature of the lower slopes. Adam Sedgwick (1785-1873), who became Professor of Geology at Trinity College, Cambridge, was a local boy, the son of the scholarly and much loved parson. A huge block of granite, on which is carved simply his name and dates, stands at a street corner to commemorate the memorable inhabitant; for he often visited Dent and remained attached to it, and to the Dalesfolk, all his life. In 1837 he came and laid the foundation stone of a new chapel in Cowgill, at the eastern end of the dale, where two of his sisters had founded a Sunday School more than thirty years before. He recalled the occasion:

The day was glorious, the face of nature beautiful and all parties in good humour and charity. About seven hundred mountaineers [sic] including nearly two hundred Sunday School children and about a hundred strangers made a curious mixed procession in the wild glen where the little chapel is now rising from the ground . . . I trust God will bless the undertaking which begins so smilingly. . . We began by making the rocks echo back the Old Hundredth Psalm, my brother read one or two short prayers. . . I handled the trowel and laid the stone and then addressed my countrymen, after which we again uncurled ourselves into a long string to the tune of God Save the King, and the strangers and schoolchildren and some others went down to Dent [nearly four miles!] and had cold meat and coffee at the Old Parsonage. My sister made thirty-six gallons of coffee in a brewing vessel. (Speakman, 1982)

This chapel, in a roundabout way, is the cause of our knowing many otherwise forgotten details of the history of Dent and its people. For Sedgwick, on discovering many years after the event recorded above that the name Cowgill had not been the name officially given to the chapel in the records of the Ecclesiastical Commissioners, set about correcting the error. The commissioners had evidently objected to the vulgar associations of Cowgill, and had wrongly named the chapel Kirkthwaite Chapel. Sedgwick proceeded to write a 'memorial' to the commissioners, requesting that the rightful name be restored. However, it was only after the intervention of Queen Victoria and Gladstone that the commissioners were forced to change the name, the royal intervention being delightfully recorded in a second publication: *Supplement to the Memorial by the Trustees of Cowgill Chapel* (1870). Attached to the memorials were a number of appendices in which he recalled many of his youthful memories of Dent and Dentdale, and referred in passing to the traditional customs, the dialect, the climate and economy of the dale. In these recollections we learn of the prosperous years enjoyed by the inhabitants, when wool from their sheep was spun and then knitted by groups of women gathered round a cottage fire, telling ghost stories or one of them reading aloud but continuing to knit, perhaps from *Robinson Crusoe*, from *Pilgrim's Progress* or the Bible. Nor did these ladies allow a walk to market to interrupt their knitting, and the stockings, mittens and caps which they sold in Kendal Market had a great reputation, and not only in the surrounding Dales.

But Sedgwick sadly recalls the decline of this little community: 'The gigantic progress of mechanical and manufacturing skill utterly crushed and swept away the little fabric of industry that had been renowned in Dent . . . the silk thread that had held society together had begun to fail and lawless manners followed.'

Today it might be said that a certain prosperity has returned to the village – but at what a price!

Dent has become a show village. It gives the impression, even out of season, of preparing itself to win the Best Kept Village Competition. Of course if you like your villages to look like the opening scene of a pantomime, then Dent on a fine day is for you. It has narrow cobbled streets, little craft and art boutiques, dainty tea shops and a couple of well-scrubbed pubs. In its favour, without a doubt, is the craftiest grass floor to its public car park I've ever driven onto.

It's interesting to compare Dent with Ingleton. Ingleton is not ashamed to be a commercial centre in its own right, while managing to live with, but not blatantly off or from, tourists and summer visitors. The Ingleton Gala is in August and is a local and rather jolly affair.

Ingleton Gala

But let's start walking from Dent. To get onto Cravens Way or the old Ribblehead packhorse path, it's necessary to make for Whernside Manor, a mile and a half east of the village. It is a large square house built in the nineteenth century. It is now given over to providing courses for cavers or climbers, and is run by the Yorkshire Dales National Park. A good shop, in an outbuilding, sells useful items of equipment for serious sportsmen, whether their pursuits take them down and under, or up and over.

If you visit the shop you can, with permission, go through the Manor grounds, following a path behind the house, up to a stile in a corner of the field; the first stile is followed almost immediately by another one which deposits you on the road you want.

Alternatively one can turn off to the right just before reaching the Manor, up a road with a Dead End sign; but after about 200 yards a green signpost, one of the many provided by the Dales National Park, indicating Bridle Path to Ribblehead brings you up a short lane to the start of Cravens Way. It starts as a pleasant, wide green road between two walls, rising gently, but not so gently that you are not totally justified, every now and then, in stopping and turning round to look at the magnificent view down Dentdale, towards Sedbergh and the Howgills with their smooth rounded tops. As you continue to climb, the right-hand wall disappears, the path veers slightly to the right and the track gets deeply rutted. If you look to the right where there is now no wall, over Deepdale, there's a lovely and huge indentation in the side of Combe Hill on the other side. It looks as though, many thousands of years ago ('Oh Best Beloved,' as the *Just So Stories* say), before the hills had hardened off, a big fat giantess had sat herself on the side of Combe Hill to rest and left her mark, and ever since that moment (and you can pinpoint the indentation on the map) that place has been called Combe Bottom. (The prosaic reality of course is that it was caused by glacial erosion.)

Ahead and slightly to the left the Settle–Carlisle railway comes into view, for once going horizontally on the same contour line. Dent Station is there, at 1,500 feet above sea level, the highest main-line station in England. It is now closed, but is a reminder that railway companies a hundred years ago served the locals well. True, the Dent locals had to walk or ride four miles from the village to get there, and climb 750 feet between the valley and the station.

725858

723858
724857

Limekilns

743847

The track continues pleasantly, a second wall appearing to make it again into a green road; there's a gate across it, the path becomes peaty, and then passes a series of springs. Old Wife's Well is on the right of the wall, and the rest are on the left, emerging where the porous peat or shale meets a bed of impervious limestone. Just before reaching a second gate across the road you can see, through a gate in the left-hand wall, the top of a large limekiln, one of the many to be found on the lower slopes of the Three Peaks and in the Dales.

In Dentdale alone, thirty old limekilns have been located; usually they are still quite prominent, although they have merged unobtrusively into the landscape. They are placed strategically, to save both time and energy. First they are sited beside a limestone outcrop occurring in the Yoredale Series; there is often evidence in the form of a little, disused quarry that the limestone they were fed with was dug out within a few feet of the kiln. Not far away, but above the opening of the kiln, there would be some source of fuel, perhaps an outcrop of coal or peat or possibly wood. And finally it would be built just above the pastures where the lime produced would eventually be carried downhill to be spread.

Most of the kilns in the area would have been built in the latter half of the 18th century, when, after the enclosures, there was a growing demand for lime to improve the new pastures. Arthur Raistrick reckons that they went out of use about the middle of the following century, when lime could be obtained more cheaply via canal or rail from more distant sources. The principle which went into the design of the field kilns was the same. The structure consisted of a heavily-built stone tower set into the slope of the hill. The top would have been open and level with the surface of the limestone outcrop. On the downhill side, a vaulted chamber would be built into the tower at ground level. The sides of the tower would be perpendicular while the inside would be shaped like an inverted cone. At the base of the cone, ending at the rear of the vaulted chamber, would be an iron grating or solid stone beams through which ash and lime could fall.

First brushwood would be thrown in at the top, followed by coal or other fuel; then the limestone rocks; then more fuel, and more rocks. This layering would continue until the top was reached, then the kiln would be fired from below. It might stay alight for as long as three days. Afterwards, the quicklime would be taken out from the open vault at the bottom, and spread on the fields below the kiln or taken away in carts.

744844   After the reference to coal, it won't come as a surprise to learn from the map that Old Coal Pits lie directly up the hill from this kiln. They, and the track leading up to them, are more clearly marked on the map than on the ground, but there is a gap in the wall on the right, where stone uprights are evidence of there having once been a gate, through which the coal was carted across Cravens Way from the pits to the kiln.

Limekiln on Penyghent

744846   This old crossroads is the point of decision for any walker still uncertain as to whether to make for the top of Whernside by going up past the old pits, or to continue, gently, along the path and down to Ribblehead. The top is still a long way off, nearly two miles as the seagull flies and 500 feet higher above the sea. And it's not easy walking. Compensations are the Whernside Tarns and, if there's no cloudcap over the top, a great view. The Tarns are easily missed, since they can be seen (even without mist and rain, which are not unusual) only when one is almost upon them. Precise instructions here are therefore useful. From the gap in the wall, looking south, the cairns at each end of the ridge ahead, called Pike, should be visible. Make for the right-hand and taller one; this route will lead past various humps and basins which must be the remains of the pits and mounds of spoil. When the right-hand cairn is reached, another one is visible ahead, with a clear path leading to it. But here there is a

740838   trap. From this second cairn a clear path leads, or rather misleads, in the same direction. Insist on taking the much less distinct path branching off half-left, which, after a couple of

740835   hundred yards, arrives at the tongue of land separating the first two tarns. The tarns are shallow and dark, surrounded by little beaches of sand and gravel and grey flat pebbles and stones. The sand, supposedly, is what the farmers used for sharpening their scythes. This is also the place where blackheaded gulls in springtime once used to come in from the coast, as the curlews still do on the lower slopes, to lay their eggs, but they were driven away, it seems, by inexpert bird watchers or possibly by mindless egg collectors. In winter the tarns are impressive because they easily freeze. On very hot summer days with little wind people have been tempted to take a dip, but such circumstances occur seldom. The third tarn is about 400 yards further ahead towards the summit and slightly to the left. Leaving it on the left, one should climb the slope called, significantly, Millstone Brow, and then over another ridge called, interestingly, Knoutberry Hill. Interesting because Knoutberry is a country name for Cloudberry, a plant much sought after but found only in the north: the flowers are white and the berries orange-red and edible (see page 142).

743836   Soon a broken-down wall leads up towards the top, met by one from the east. Climb over where they meet and follow the path along the ridge to the cairn and the trig point.

738815 From the summit, one way down is the direct steep route facing Park Fell. For those who like sliding it's fun for a while, but to avoid acute discomfort and an almost perpendicular drop it is worth going a little further along the ridge in the direction of Ingleton before starting down. A much better way is to go back along the wall followed after the tarns, but after a few

743823 hundred yards to branch off down the slope to Greensett Tarn. It's very marshy around the tarn and there is little or no sign of a

748823 path, but it's worth aiming for Coal Gill and noting some more old coal pits on the right of the stream. Coal Gill soon joins

757823 Force Gill, alongside which there is a well-worn path. This leads

761818 past a couple of impressive waterfalls and joins Cravens Way just before it reaches the railway.

Park Fell

For those who decided that discretion was the better part of the valour needed to get to the top, we'll start again at that

744846

limekiln. Instead of turning right past the old coal pits and up to the Whernside Tarns and the summit, one can save energy and keep straight on along a pleasantly horizontal path. After less than a mile it swings right along a stream. The path becomes obscure here, but when great banks of peat appear ahead one

751837

needs to bear left before reaching them, and continue alongside the peat until the green track becomes clear again and starts to go downhill. It is here, if anywhere, that one thinks again of Jacquetta Hawkes's conquering Romans and their cambered road with its culverts, but I'm inclined to think scepticism will prevail, even though the path here becomes as straight as a Roman road all the way down to the railway. In fact I'd advise deviating from the path and aiming for Force Gill, which can be seen ahead and to the right; as indicated above, it is an impressive ravine with some fine waterfalls. Before going too far down it's worth looking over onto Blea Moor to the left, where two huge piles of stones can be seen. They were hauled up through the airshafts of the famous Blea Moor Tunnel (2640 yards long) when it was made in the early 1870s. These piles of stones, raised laboriously by steam winches from the tunnel workings, form strange cones on the hillside.

Tank for steam engines (now demolished) at Blea Moor sidings

Before reaching the railway at a point about ¼ mile from the mouth of the tunnel the path goes alongside Force Gill and then path and stream cross the line together. This makes the bridge into an aqueduct, a surprising piece of civil engineering. It's especially surprising since no sooner has the stream been channelled over the line by the aqueduct than it is taken under it again through another bridge carrying the railway. Surely the engineers could have had a new water course dug or blasted on the west side of the line and saved the building of the aqueduct over it. However, the aqueduct remains a remarkable engineering achievement.

761816

There is still another mile to go along the east side of the line, which now goes down Littledale from where the great blocks of limestone for the Ribblehead Viaduct were quarried. The path down isn't very exciting. It passes the Blea Moor sidings, which not long ago used to offer some delight to industrial archaeologists. Here the great rectangular water tank was to be seen lying proudly on the top of a stout brick structure; there were

757806

the remains of buffers and pipes and pumps, where the steam locomotives would top up after panting up the 'Long Drag' from Settle station. But these relics have now been tidied away by British Rail, leaving only the still-functioning signal box and a few good stories about happenings on the line.

One of the signalmen who used to man the Blea Moor Box was a keen fisherman. He used to make flies for himself with bits of feather and thin wire. He became an expert and eventually much sought-after as a supplier. When engine drivers who were also fishermen needed to replenish their stock, they would give a coded series of hoots as they passed the Horton Signal Box, a few miles down the line. The Horton man would telephone Blea Moor, and our fisherman–cum–signalman would divert the train onto his siding where it would stop, ostensibly for the driver to take on water, but in fact to collect a small tobacco tin full of skilfully made flies, and to hand over a few shillings in return.

The path beside the line leads down beside the twenty-four arches of Batty Moss Viaduct, as it was first called, over the lumpy, marshy waste of Batty Green.

The Settle–Carlisle Railway

766793 And here we are at Ribblehead. It's impossible here not to wonder about the shanty towns of over two thousand men, women and children who lived here in wooden huts, some for three or more years between 1870 and 1874, while the tunnel and the viaduct were being built. Probably the men who today wander purposefully across the Moss at weekends with metal detectors are wondering too, but they don't really get any closer to those drunken Anglo-Irish fights, the deaths from accidents and disease, or the engineering feats which these marshes witnessed just over a hundred years ago. For the navvies had to be tough. Some had built railways across America – hence Salt Lake as a name of one of their shanty towns, which still sticks today to the row of Railway Cottages off the Horton Road near Ribblehead. These were built in 1874 for the staff maintaining the line; the nearby quarry has the name of Salt Lake also attached to it, but today it yields only vegetation, and is the preserve of the Yorkshire Naturalists' Trust, and a rather fierce notice by the railway bridge warns all but card-carrying naturalists to keep out (see page 118).

Some of the railway navvies had no doubt fought or built railways in the Crimea, hence Sebastapol and Inkerman, the names of shanty villages on the lower slopes of Blea Moor. There were others. A superior one where the engineers lived was called Belgravia, and two more higher up the slope were called Jerusalem and Jericho, a reminder that a Scripture reader was provided for the shanty town by the railway company, which later also provided a policeman, a schoolmaster and a hospital with a doctor.

In the summer of 1870 there were 6000 men working on the whole project, many living all the year round with their families in the shanty towns along the route, some lodging at Selside and Chapel le Dale, some coming daily from surrounding farms. Fights and accidents could be fatal, as could the smallpox epidemic which went through the 'town' of Batty Green in 1871. Five people died in one week and were buried at Chapel le Dale. There were many deaths; one estimate puts it at over a hundred workmen alone, but the records in Chapel le Dale church also show many deaths among women and children. They cannot all have been buried there, even though the burial ground was extended, the Midland Railway contributing £20 towards the cost. No graves of railwaymen are to be found in the churchyard today, but a small memorial tablet in the chapel commemorates those who died 'on the railway'.

The Settle-Carlisle was the last great mainline railway to be built in this country, comprising seventy-two miles of track, twenty major viaducts and fourteen tunnels. Neither from an economic nor from a national point of view was it a necessary enterprise, but it was magnificent and reflected the pride and confidence of Victorian economic adventurers. The Midland Railway was a great and powerful company, but it had no through route, with its own track all the way, between London and Scotland. The directors refused to 'stand idly by' and allow this lucrative and prestigious traffic to be monopolised by the LNER and LNWR. A purely Midland line was the only policy they could favour.

James Allport became a director of the company in 1857 at the age of 46; in 1860 he became General Manager, and remained in the post till 1880. He was a typical Railway King, combining his interest in railways with shipbuilding. (He was a director of Palmers in Jarrow.) In the autumn of 1865, this solid respectable middle-aged member of the capitalist establishment set off on

foot from Settle, accompanied by the company's Chief
Engineer, John Crosby, and walked up to Ribblehead, over Blea
Moor, on past Appleby and most of the way to Carlisle. In spite
of foul weather and peat bogs and an almost total lack of roads,
they decided that the plan to build a double track railway line
along this route was feasible.

There was much ensuing uncertainty and considerable
opposition from shareholders, mainly because of the cost to the
company, estimated at one and a half million pounds. Critics
said it would need double the sum and even they under-
estimated. The first stretch of line to be built was from Settle to
Dent Head. The surveyors arrived in 1869 and ten of them spent
the winter in a four-wheeled caravan at Ribblehead. By July of
the following summer a hundred wooden huts, solidly
constructed, were standing on Batty Green, the marshy stretch
which lies just north of the Ribblehead T-junction today. A
tramway, a narrow gauge railway, was laid out, 4 miles of it in
all, to carry material along the route which the line would take,

up to Blea Moor. The embankments and levelled surfaces used by the tram line are today the only physical reminders of this amazing temporary invasion. At one time Batty Green had a population of 2000!

Here all sorts of workshops were set up. Blacksmiths, carpenters, masons all needed working accommodation. The brickworks were at Sebastapol, near to where the viaduct now stands; there were ten ovens which could produce 20,000 bricks per day. They were needed to line the tunnel and the arches of the viaduct. But unskilled navvies made up the bulk of the work force; by the summer of 1870 there were 1400 men and 170 horses working on this first stretch of line, most of them concerned with the viaduct and the tunnel. Bog carts were used for transporting materials, pulled by heavy shire horses, and fitted with barrels in place of wheels, to stop them sinking. The foundations of the piers of the viaduct were laid on solid rock, but they had to dig through 25 feet of mud and clay to get to it. The great blocks of stone were quarried in nearby Littledale and Salt Lake; the biggest one weighed 8 tons.

By the time the contract was nearing completion the conditions in the huts and outside them became horrifying. The local Medical Officer of Health wrote that:

> The wooden huts, occupied by navvies, miners, their families and lodgers are clustered upon a patch of bogland made almost untraversable by reason of the state of puddle it is in from surface water and refuse matter thrown out immediately from the doorways. . . There is no vestige of drainage save the open trenches cut round the walls of the huts to protect them from inundation. . . In one hut I noticed five bedsteads jammed so tightly together that the sleepers in reaching the furthest beds must necessarily clamber over the others. There was no provision for a separation of the sexes.

Illegal drinking was the main crime, and drunkenness was very common; and there were fierce fights between the English and Irish navvies, the former refusing to work alongside the latter. In 1870 the Ingleton magistrates convicted Mary Ann Lea, a widow of 32, who had 'danced in indecent manner' with drunken navvies at the Hill Inn.

On 3 August 1875 the first freight train travelled over the line; on 1 May 1876 the first regular passenger train completed the journey.

It is still one of the classic railway lines of England. It offers unparalleled views, so that one wonders why observation cars have never been put into service. Regularly in the early 1980s special steam trains travel the line on certain Sundays, packed with enthusiasts. Enthusiasts also line the track, aiming their cameras at the passing giant. A regular passenger and goods service is still operating, but many small stations have been closed and sold or simply destroyed. After the great initiative of its construction, the story in these later years has been sad and will almost certainly become sadder.

The great viaduct at Ribblehead with its 24 arches and 100-foot piers is crumbling. Judgement is reserved (1982) but the sentence will almost certainly be closure. A replacement would cost nearly £5 million, and the cost of maintaining it throughout the 1970s was £600,000. And it was in a worse condition at the end of the decade than at the beginning. The winds, syphoned along the valley from the west, and sometimes reaching 120 mph, have done most of the damage to the stonework and mortar; frost has done the rest, with rainwater seeping into the piers from the top and then freezing. Perhaps we shouldn't blame the hundred-year-old viaduct as much as the 300-million-year-old limestone: for it is this which is reaching its allotted span.

In a museum-conscious age maybe the structure will still be allowed to stand; but without trains going across it, its function will have gone and the beauty of architecture has much to do with function. It's still a great sight, especially on a summer evening with the Carlisle express streaking across it. Those of us who carry memories of such events can be grateful.

Easter Sunday

It was a blue and silver morning and I was woken by the sheep scratching their necks on the gate. I got up and was suddenly tuned in to an orchestra of birdsong. The noisiest were the starlings; three of them seemed to be playing tig between the trees. I got up, pulled on clothes and wandered over the rocks towards the wood. The grass was still frost-white but the tops of the rocks had thawed out and the tight-fitting moss and saxifrage glistened cheerfully bright green. The aconites hadn't opened yet, but just occasionally in the grass between the rocks there were some shy and modest little single primroses – no big clumps of them here, possibly because the sheep eat them. The birds were keeping up a continuous chirruping and whistling and then a woodpigeon joined in. The woodwind? It sounded like a soft repetitive oboe.

I climbed over the cliff barrier into the wood. It was enchanted. The sun struck the trees (and me) horizontally. The wreckage of many a winter storm lies under moss and grassy covers exactly where it fell. There are no giants here, but one big ash lay prostrate, and where it had once been growing, it raised a huge root upwards, awkwardly. But the sense of life going on was strong and even emphasised – trees growing out of cracks in rocks, whole hedges of new thin branches growing out of the inert horizontal trunk of a fallen sycamore; it had managed to stay connected to the world by some of its bent-over roots; and between rocks, in the deep grykes where it was warmer than where I stood, all kinds of greenery was pushing its way up. I looked into a little dell, enclosed by the black sides of huge rocks; growing there I thought I had found a carpet of about-to-flower Lily of the Valley. *Porte-bonheur*, I thought ('Bringer of luck' – that's why it's a May Day gift), and I jumped down to look closer and was struck through the nostrils by the smell of salad dressing! Wild garlic, of course, whose leaves do look like Lily of the Valley when they are young. The real name is Ramsoms, though around here they call them stink rods. I moved over some more rocks towards the cliff edge, a natural defensive wall against incursion from the pasture below, and a protecting wall for the sheep feeding there. An old iron bed-end had been put across a possible point of entry to stop sheep; it was rusting away. I wondered what births and deaths it had witnessed. . . Next to it a fallen bird-cherry tree had been placed to add to the defences. But a little further on, evidence of failure. In a fissure between two rocks nestling so comfortably, head on its side, and its whole woolly body packed closely between the rock sides, a dead sheep. Probably it had wandered in during the last big snowfall a month ago, when the pass into the wood had been undefended, smoothed over with hard snow. It had slipped down five feet, and stayed there cold and bleating.

Around the rim of the slit where it was, bits of wool were scattered – wisps collected by the nesting birds to make things comfortable; and I was suitably reminded of Easter, the dead sheep serving the live birds, providing the family with a soft warm place to be born in. 'Except the seed die. . .'

I walked on a little way and found myself looking down on the Druid's Altar Stone. I climbed down. The little ash tree growing out of the forehead of the flat frowning face of the priest's rock beside the altar was in bud. It was larger than last year, and the huge rounded rocks surrounding the place of sacrifice looked quite friendly with the sun full in their faces. I noticed a new yellow, a golden yellow moss slapped like paint on the lower part of one of these by-standers.

I walked slowly back along the meadow, disturbing some of the rare rabbits which had been playing there, and sent them scuttling into the slits in the rocks. And so towards the wall and the stile, where a couple of wagtails, so effectively camouflaged into the black and grey of the stones, made themselves obvious, silly birds, by their ever vibrating tails. Over the stile, over the field and up the track to wake my guests and make breakfast. . .

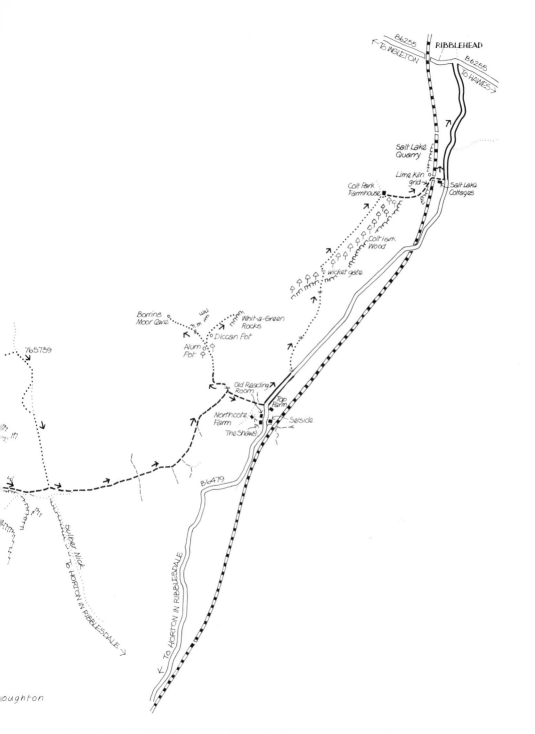

B6255
RIBBLEHEAD
← TO INGLETON
B6255
TO HAWES →

Salt Lake
Quarry

Lime Kiln
grid

Colt Park
Farmhouse

Salt Lake
Cottages

Colt Park
Wood

wicket gate

Barrins
Moor Cave

Whit-a-Green
Rocks

Diccan Pot

765739

Alum
Pot

Old Reading
Room

Top
Farm

Northcote
Farm

Selside

The Shaws

B6479

Sulber Nick
TO HORTON IN RIBBLESDALE

TO HORTON IN RIBBLESDALE

oughton

Water-worn rock near
Ribblehead

80

Chapter 3: Clapham Village to Ribblehead by the Side of Ingleborough

Clapham is a good place either to start or to finish a walk. For many years, in fact, it has been recognised as 'a good place'. J.S. Fletcher, in his *Picturesque History of Yorkshire*, 1899, wrote: 'In spite of the annual incursion of sightseers, Clapham is still in possession of its ancient charm, and many folk would give a good deal to settle down for ever amidst its pastoral quietudes.' The annual incursion, which he noted, arose: 'because the Railway Folk began conveying so many tourists to Clapham. . . Its greatest attraction perhaps lies in the view which one gets of it from the railway line, from whose formal preciseness it is conveniently set apart.'

Set apart indeed it is, lying a mile and a quarter from the village: carless tourists still use it to come to Clapham, and Clapham is still 'in possession of its ancient charm'. There are few houses in the main part which are less than 150 years old, and the newer ones are not obtrusive. There are only two shops, one of which is also the Post Office, and two cafés. The offices of *The Dalesman* are modestly tucked away up a snicket. They are worth visiting, for this modest little publishing house not only brings out its pocket-size illustrated magazine every month, which goes to subscribers all over the world (to 60,000 of them in 1980), but is responsible for numerous popular and scholarly publications, which are displayed and on sale in these rural offices.

A country pottery operates in the former village smithy. The original furnace, with its rebuilt chimney, serves today to heat a hypocaust where the local clay is gently dried after washing. On sunny days, in the yard open to the road, one can see recently turned pots and puncheons put out to dry on tables and shelves before being fired. And this final process turns them from a muddy yellow to a warm flowerpot red.

This is one of the very few commercial potteries in the country which uses local clay dug out from the nearby hillside by the potters themselves. They wash and dry it themselves too. It's hard work, but worth it, and not only from an economic point of view – they get satisfaction from it as well as from potting. It's a reminder that Burton in Lonsdale, not three miles from Clapham, just below the Craven Fault, was once a centre for ceramics, and there are several abandoned potteries in the area. For clay is generally found lying with coal measures, and just as the Staffordshire coalfield explains the Potteries (providing not only clay but the means of firing), so the Ingleton coal measures did the same.

Clapham Beck, a sizable stream, divides the village lengthways down the middle, and is bounded on each bank by a separate road. Three stone bridges connect the two roadways, the middle one for pedestrians only, with a fine single arch. There is today only one pub in the village itself, the New Inn. There is another pub, over a mile away, opposite the little station called the Flying Horseshoe. The name derives from the

family crest of the Farrers (a horseshoe with wings). They have been Lords of the Manor for more than a century. There was once a third pub, beside the Post Office, with an equally peculiar name, the Bull and Cave, which Walter White, in his *Month in Yorkshire*, 1858, thought must be a mistake. Like Fletcher, later, he was entranced by Clapham:

> It is adorned with flowers and climbers and smooth grass plots, embowered by trees and watered by a merry brook, lying open to the sun on the roots of Ingleborough. Looking about for an inn I saw the Bull and Cave and secured quarters for myself by leaving my knapsack. Bull and Cave seemed to me such an odd coupling that I fancied that Cave must be a Yorkshire way of spelling calf; but it really means what it purports, and the two words are yoked together in order that visitors, who are numerous, may be easily attracted.

Finally the Old Reading Room, on the left bank of the Beck, is worth noticing not only for what it is, but for what it was. On the first floor the Yorkshire Dales National Park has established a very fine National Park Centre, where maps and useful guides are sold, exhibitions mounted and information about the area is given. Reading Rooms were once a feature of the Dales. They were provided sometimes by the Chapel, sometimes (as in the North Riding) by a philanthropic mining company, or, as is the case at Clapham, by the Lord of the Manor. Here books and newspapers were made available for the village; indeed underneath the National Park Centre a room still serves as a common room for the village.

The building itself was once the Manor House, inhabited by the Inglebys who bought the manor from the Claphams in the 16th century. The lintel over the old front door is curiously carved and the lettering, **WCI 1701**, is still clearly readable. In the Middle Ages the family of Clapham was given the manor by Henry II. Their seat was Clapdale Castle, which dominated the village where Clapdale Farm now stands. The family gets a brief mention in Wordsworth's 'White Doe of Rylstone', where he pictures the corpses of the Claphams in the vault of the chapel at Bolton Abbey:

> . . . through the chink in the fractured floor
> Look down and see a grisley sight
> A vault where the bodies are buried upright!
> There face by face and hand by hand
> The Claphams and Mauleverers stand.

The reason for this tiring position is said to be that Claphams would bow to no man, living or dead, and Wordsworth recalls one of them, John-de-Clapham, who, in the Wars of the Roses:

Dragged Earl Pembroke from Banbury Church
And smote off his head on the stones of the porch.

There is also a local legend that John's foster-mother, Alice Kettyl, sold her soul to the devil and became a witch. She was thereby able to find him an extra five hundred horse to go and fight on the Lancastrian side in the Wars of the Roses.

Since the early years of the 18th century, the Farrer family have been associated with Clapham. Oliver Farrer (1742-1808) built up the family fortunes, and over the years bought land and shooting rights in the neighbourhood. He was a frugal man, and is reputed, in order no doubt to save the fare, to have walked from Clapham to London. In London, where he was articled to a firm of solicitors, he was known as Penny Bun Farrer to his fellow clerks. But he became senior partner before he retired to Clapham. His fortune and extensive property enabled his nephew James (1812-1879) to buy the manorial rights. James and his younger brother, also called Oliver, organised the planting of numerous trees alongside the upper reaches of Clapham Beck. In 1840 they built a new Manor House, on the foundations of a former shooting lodge. They called it Ingleborough Hall, which stands solidly today just off the road at the head of the village. It is the only house for miles around which could be described as a stately home, for although it dates from Victorian times, it bears a distant relationship to those grand country seats built in the previous century by the Wentworths and Fitzwilliams a hundred miles further south. It is faced with smooth rectangular blocks of stone and, though only one storey high, has an imposing facade overlooking the lawn in which the remains of a fountain are still to be seen. A domed apse juts out onto the terrace, some of the high windows of which are still fitted with the original curved glass panes. The semi-circular pediment is supported by four Doric pillars, while the heavy traditional pediment over the front door, round the corner from the terrace, is also supported by Doric pillars and two simple pilasters. Inside the front door the entrance hall is distinguished by the pillars and circular staircase made of 'Dent Marble', a greenish grey limestone which, when polished, is patterned all over with crinoid fossils (see page 55). The original furniture has been removed, but the Adam-type marble fireplaces are still there, and lovely heavy mahogany doors, some of which are curved to match the shape of the room, swing on their brass hinges as silently as when they were made.

Two features of the house are worth special mention; first the tunnel, wide and high and 200 yards long, lit only by two small skylights; it leads from a road which skirts the property to the servants' entrance, the servants being expected to pass through this rather frightening tunnel when walking between the village and the house, so they should not be seen by the owners or their guests. It must be the most singular and stony-hearted servants' entrance in the country. Secondly there is the Ice House, built into the hill at the back of the house. It is a round windowless chamber, 30 feet deep and 18 feet across. It was filled every winter with ice from the frozen lake a hundred yards away and was used, among other things, to provide cold drinks for the family during the occasional hot days of summer.

By 1945 the Hall and the grounds were in a bad state, and the family was pleased to sell it for £6000 to the West Riding Education Authority, to be used as a Special School. They restored the fabric of the building, and today it is used by a consortium of most of the smaller education authorities into which the West Riding was carved up in 1973. It serves as an Outdoor Education Centre with its own teaching and support staff. About 60 children a week come there from the industrial towns of Yorkshire, and are occasionally to be seen eagerly exploring and studying the caves and potholes, the fossils and flowers, bird and beasts of this wild and unspoilt landscape.

In the 1830s, the nephews of Penny Bun Farrer, James and Oliver, had the idea of damming Clapham Beck above the village to form the half-mile-long eight-acre ornamental lake, extending what had been known as Clapham Tarn. On the south side the lake is contained by high limestone cliffs, and along the north side, which slopes gently down to the lakeside, a gradually rising path, Clapdale Drive, leads between the trees. It's wide enough for all the carriages which no doubt conveyed ladies and gentlemen from the hall up as far as the impressive Ingleborough Cave (which lies about a mile and a half from the village) and even further on to Trow Gill. A bridge carries a private drive across the dam from the hall to the lakeside path, and family privacy was also preserved (as in the case of the servants' entrance mentioned above) by the building of two

more tunnels to take Thwaite Lane, a public bridlepath, underneath the grounds of the estate.

But it is another member of the Farrer family, Reginald John (1881-1920), who is probably the best known. He was an Edwardian all-rounder; author of long-forgotten novels and historical romances, explorer and travel writer (*The Garden of Asia* was his first book), a failed politician (he stood for parliament as a Liberal), a convert to Buddhism, a skilful flower-painter and, above all, a botanist who combined plant-collecting in the course of his many journeys abroad with practical gardening. Educated at home in Clapham, he walked extensively and intensively as a boy around Ingleborough, and at the age of 14 started a rock garden in a disused quarry in the grounds of the Hall. (The garden is now overgrown, and is in fact no longer in the grounds of the present property.)

He read Greats at Oxford, and then went off to travel in
Japan, Korea and China. After this he concentrated on botanical
journeys in the Alps, but in 1913 he set out for Tibet and China
on a plant-hunting expedition. He returned home in 1915,
worked in the Ministry of Information and, straight after the
war, went out again to the Far East, being based in Upper
Burma. Here he succumbed to the climate, died and was buried.
It was immediately after the war that his magnum opus of 1000
pages, *The English Rock Garden*, was published. Here he
attempted to classify and describe every known rock plant
worth growing. His own garden at the Hall had by then become
famous and was much visited. He was a naturalist in more
senses than one, for he abhorred the romantic and fantastic
shapes which people tried to achieve with rocks. In his book he
referred scathingly to some such attempts as 'the Almond

Pudding', 'the Dog's Grave' and 'the Drunkard's Dream'. His own precepts were in favour of following the natural stratifications and contours of the surrounding rocks. Among the plants, he introduced from Switzerland a rare species of gentian about which he wrote that 'it was well worth the two whole years' expedition', and also shrubs from the Far East: *Viburnum fragrans, Clematis macropetela,* and *Potentilla fructiosa.*

Reginald would send back to Clapham specimens and seeds of plants that he had found in Burma and in the foothills of the Himalayas. He also sent specimens to experts at Kew Gardens. The latter noticed that the gardener at Clapham was often more successful than they were at raising the seeds and seedlings, in spite of their hothouse expertise. For his own gardener at the Hall decided to make use of the ice pit there for purposes other than making cool drinks. His trick, the experts eventually discovered, was to cover his cold frames with blocks of ice in the winter months, making the Himalayan plants feel quite at home. When the warmer weather came, he removed the ice, or it melted, and the plants happily sprouted and sent out shoots.

Reginald was essentially practical. He wanted to establish certain plants on the cliff face on the south side of Clapham Tarn, to make a kind of hanging garden of Clapham. The cliff was not scalable. He therefore took a boat onto the lake, replaced the shot in his cartridges with seeds and fired them into the crevices of the cliff. Some, as was to be expected, fell on stony ground and among thorns, but some fell on good ground and brought forth fruit, and flowers. Since he was buried in Burma, at his own request, a simple plinth with the flying horseshoe carved on it stands beside a path in the grounds of Ingleborough Hall, and a memorial garden is being re-established around it, containing many of the species he introduced into this country.

Reginald's father, another James (1849-1926), was equally ingenious. He made use of the head of water formed by the artificial lake to drive an early form of turbo-generator, which was made by Gilks and Gordon of Kendal in 1890. It is still in working order in the shed below the dam, and provides power for the saw-mill where once bobbins were turned for Yorkshire textile mills, but which now serves the Ingleborough estate. In the early days, electricity thus generated made it possible for the tenants in the village to have electric light, each house being allowed one carbon filament bulb; furthermore the benevolent landlord arranged for the village streets to be electrically lit, so that Clapham became one of the first villages in the north-west to be lit by electricity.

The Farrer line remains unbroken. The present Lord of the Manor, Dr John Farrer, succeeded to the estate in 1953, hearing of his unexpected inheritance while working as a doctor in Australia. He had had no thoughts of becoming a landowner, but he came, saw and was conquered; for he liked the prospect, taught himself estate management and agriculture, and has built up a flourishing rural community in and around the village. One example of his far-sighted planning is his policy, when one of his houses becomes vacant, of favouring couples who are actual or potential parents of young children. The village school remains not merely open, but full.

Beck Head Cave

But now for walking. The easiest and most civilised way out
of the village is to take the gently sloping path beside the lake,
leading up to Ingleborough Cave. There was a time when the
reigning Farrer put it out of bounds to visitors. Walter White,
visiting the cave in 1850, had to make a detour, following the
rather steep and rutted lane leading up to Clapdale Farm. He
first secured the services of a guide in the village:

746696

> The guide, an old soldier, and a good specimen of the class,
> civil and intelligent, called first at his house as we passed, to
> get candles. Below us on the right lay cultivated grounds and
> well kept plantations through which, as the old man told me,
> visitors were once allowed to walk on their way to the cave –
> a pleasing and less toilsome way than the lane, but the
> remains of picnics left on the grass, broken bottles, orange
> peels, greasy paper and wisps of hay became such a serious
> abuse of the privilege that Mr Farrer withdrew his
> permission. 'It's a wonder to me', said the guide 'that people
> shouldn't know how to behave themselves.' (*A Month in
> Yorkshire*, 1858)

Today's walkers, better disciplined, are allowed to take the
once forbidden path. It's a truly pleasurable experience, and
indeed a strange surprise for anyone who has been walking over
the open fells and limestone pavements of the surrounding
countryside on previous days. Here one is transported to the
graceful living of the 18th century, and surely this is what James
and Oliver wanted to reproduce when they planned this
landscaped drive halfway through the nineteenth.

At the top of the village is the sawmill and timber yard
through which walkers have to pass to gain access to the path. A
further necessity is to call at the sawmill cottage to pay a modest
fee for the privilege of walking through the well-kept private
grounds. Here too a useful booklet, *The Reginald Farrer Nature
Trail*, can be bought.

It would be possible just to walk up the wide path beside the
lake without taking special notice of the trees, but it would be
difficult. They are distributed with what appears to be a kind of
deliberate randomness. In the spring, on the far side of the lake,
the new green of the beech trees stands out, almost dazzling,
against the dark evergreen pines, while the path itself is bounded
on both sides by larch and yew, oak and beech, and silver firs.
The trees are set off, in late April or early May, not only by the

green undergrowth, but by great random patches of closely packed bluebells, and by the white flowers of the wild garlic. And suddenly, near the path, among the bluebells there are little blue spikes – patches of bugle. They go on flowering long after the bluebells are dead and gone. Bugle evidently has nothing to do with trumpets, but the name is connected with the apothecary's *bugula* (a cure against melancholy), which also gives its name to Viper's Bugloss. It's an unfortunate name for a fine little plant with its cone of dark blue flowerlets; the Austrian name is surely preferable: *Blauer Kirchturm* – Blue Steeple.

The path becomes steeper towards the end of the lake, and Clapham Beck careers over rocks at the bottom of a steep slope. In early May, at this point, bamboo bushes and huge trees of rhododendron emerge on the right on both sides of the stream – their blooms, some red, some pale, burst out against their dark green leaves. No wild flowers these, but planted, many of them by Reginald Farrer, as were the bamboos. These are evidence of his expertise, for he realised that the rhododendrons would 'take' in this spot, clear of the almost ubiquitous limestone (which they hate), because at this point the slatey, lime-free and very ancient Ordovician rock pushed itself through the limestone crust and provides the acid soil in which rhododendrons flourish.

A shallow stream, Cat Hole Syke, goes under the path about here, and just below the bridge the Ordovician rocks are proudly exposed, but standing on end, pushed up to a vertical position from the level plane on which they were originally laid down. A little further on, on the left of the path, a huge stone shelter has been erected, known as the Grotto – a simple folly, shaped as an apse, with the front made from oddly formed lumps of limestone; this surely dates from the time the path was laid down; from here ladies and gentlemen could enjoy the tamed beauty of ordered woodland.

Soon the woods give way to pastures, and the path meets the stream. The rhythmic banging of a ram pump comes from a low shed beside the stream. This ingenious machine, activated by the water from the beck, pushes that same water uphill to Clapdale Farm, 100 feet up above the woods.

The principle of the ram was discovered by Pascal (1623-1664). The water from the stream passes through a lower chamber and out through a waste pipe until it gains sufficient

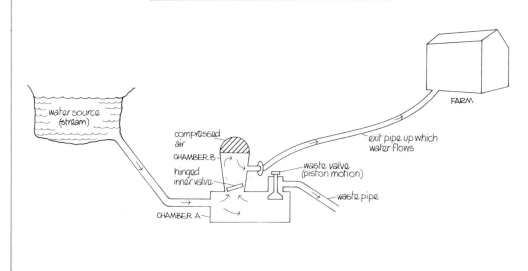

THE RAM PUMP AT CLAPDALE FARM

water source (stream)

compressed air

CHAMBER B

hinged inner valve

CHAMBER A

waste valve (piston motion)

exit pipe up which water flows

waste pipe

FARM

speed to close the waste valve. It then changes course, being pushed up through an inner valve at the top of the chamber into a second enclosed chamber. Here the air is compressed, the water loses momentum, the inner valve is closed, allowing the water to be 'rammed' up the supply pipe all the way to Clapdale Farm. Pressure in the second chamber drops, and the whole process begins again.

A few hundred yards further on, tucked away on the left, the entrance to Ingleborough Cave comes into view. William Dobson, in his *Rambles by the Ribble*, 1864, describes it as 'the most wonderful cave in England. The entrance is beneath an overhanging rock, on which were growing numberless hazels, mountain ash and elms, the beetling limestone overhead projecting like the front of an Elizabethan house.' On the occasion of his visit, having been forced to go round the long way because of previous picnic parties and their debris (see above) he reported that:

> A picnic party was at the gate of the cave, and a little flirting was going on as is customary on such occasions. In a while the janitor of the cave appeared, leading a party whom he had conducted through the interior, each bearing a candle in a

754711

rude wooden candlestick. They had been in about an hour, and on their return each member of the exploring party were loud in expressions of admiration of the wonders of the interior. Those waiting outside were now admitted, each presented with a candle, and so we entered the dim region.

The entrance to the cave has not changed in over a hundred years, nor really the behaviour of visitors, though it must be admitted that the path by the lake and the walk up to the cave are remarkably free from litter. The cave is still rightly famous. For not only does it stretch into the depths of Ingleborough Hill, but it offers the visitor new to caves a spectacular and informative experience. For the expert caver, who is prepared to crawl along wet muddy passages (called 'wallows') and swim through cold dark lakes of clear water, it offers the opportunity for rare exploration and discovery. (Special permission and expert guidance are of course necessary for these latter speleological adventures.)

Like the Whitescar Cave (see page 31) which lies, with its well-stocked shop and large car park, just off the Ingleton-Ribblehead road, this also is a pay-cave, and visitors must go in with a guide. But here similarities stop. Whitescar Cave is interesting but frankly commercial, and appeals to those who arrive in cars or coaches and like to avoid walking, while Ingleborough rewards those who have walked the mile and a half to the entrance with an experience suited to those who enjoy the natural and extraordinary, without cosmetics.

The cave passage along which one walks was once the bed of Clapham Beck, but the stream now issues from a sister cave, Beck Head, a few yards up the track and is crossed by a somewhat ornamental bridge, which no doubt once permitted Farrer guests to be taken in their carriages up beyond the cave to view the wonders of Trow Gill.

The first 60 yards of the cave were all that was explorable until the year 1837. Before that date a wall of stalagmites five feet high held back a great sheet of water, whose surface was only a few inches from the flat ceiling. Following a great flood in 1837, when the waters of the underground lake overflowed, Mr James Farrer got his gardener to chip away the stalagmite barrier and (presumably gradually!) release the pent-up waters. The two ends of the barrier are still to be seen on either side of the path and, at about 5 feet from the ground, the water mark left by the surface of the old lake is still detectable. The existence of this lake is responsible also for the first remarkable feature of the cave, the 'Inverted Forest'. Before the waters were released, short stalactites formed above the surface of the lake. But they would not penetrate the water, and so a kind of crystalised lime, tufa (see page 29), grew in a bulbous lump at the end of each stalactite, giving the impression of a bushy tree stuck upside down on the ceiling.

This and other peculiarities of the cave, including a plan and explanation of its origin and development, are given in a useful short guide by Trevor Ford (1979) which can be bought in the little store at the cave entrance. But other writers in Victorian times have described the cave more romantically, if less scientifically, and among these, Walter White, in his *Month in Yorkshire*, 1858, gave a long account of his visit; here he has just passed the stalagmite barrier:

> An involuntary exclamation broke from me as I entered and beheld what might be taken for a glittering fairy palace. On each side, sloping gently upwards till they met the roof, great bulging masses of stalagmite of snowy whiteness lay outspread, mound after mound glittering as with a million diamonds. All the great white masses are damp; their surfaces are rough with countless crystalised convolutions and minute ripples between which trickle here and there tiny threads of water. . . A strange delusion came over me as I paced slowly past the undulating ranges, and for a moment they seemed to represent the great rounded snowfields that whiten the sides of the Alps.
>
> The cavern widens; we are in Pillar Hall; stalactites of all dimensions hang from the roof, singly or in groups. Thousands are mere nipples, an inch or two in length; many are two or three feet, and the whole place resounds with the drip and tinkle of water. Stalagmites dot the floor, and while some have grown upwards the stalactites have grown downwards until the ends meet.
>
> Although geologists explain the process of formation, there is yet much food for wonder in remembering that all these various objects were formed by running water. The water, finding its way through fissures in the mighty bed of limestone overhead, hangs in drops, one drop pushes another off, but not idly; for while the current of air blowing through carries off their carbonic acid, they give up the salt of lime gathered during percolation and form small stony tubes. And

these tubes, the same cause continuing to operate, grow in the course of ages to magnificent stalactites.

Among the stalagmites are a few of beehive shape; but there is one named the Jockey Cap, an extraordinary specimen for bigness. Its base has a circumference of ten feet; its height is two feet, all produced by a succession of drops from one single point. In six years, from 1845 to 1851, the diameter increased by two, and the height by three inches. [The Jockey Cap measurement game is hilariously unscientific, and deductions regarding growth are not to be trusted. Trevor Ford states that measurements in 1967 suggest that it had grown only $\frac{1}{2}$ inch higher in 63 years.]

Then we came to a bend where the roof rushing down appears to bar all further advance, but the guide puts a thing into your hand, which you might take to be a scrubbing brush and telling you to stoop, creeps into a low entrance between the rising floor and descending roof, and you

Ingleborough from Simon Fell

discover that the scrubbing brush is a paddle to enable you to walk on three legs while crouching down. It keeps your right hand from the slippery rock; your left has always enough to do in holding the candle. . . The tunnel leads you to the Giant's Hall, where stalactites and draperies again meet your eyes, and where your light is all too feeble to illumine the lofty roof. And here is the end, 2,106 feet from the entrance – nearly half a mile. From the time the gardener broke through the barrier in the Old Cave, two years were spent in gradual advances till the Giant's Hall was reached. Adventurous explorers endeavoured to get further, for two small holes were discovered leading downwards from one side of the hall to a lower cave. They braved the danger, and let themselves down to a level where they were stopped by a deep pool. It must have looked fearfully dismal. Yet, might there not be caverns still more wonderful beyond? Fixing a candle to his cap, and with a rope round his body, Mr James Farrer swam across the murky lake, but found it closed by what appeared to be an impassable wall of limestone – the heart of Ingleborough. It was a courageous adventure. . . .

Mr Farrer's precautions against mischief have prevented that pillage of the interior so much to be deplored in other caves of the region. Yet even here some of the smaller stalactites, the size of a finger, have been missed after a party have gone through; and once a man struck a group of stalactites and broke more than a foot off the longest in sheer wantonness, it seemed, for the fragment was too large to be carried away. And there the mutilation remains, a lasting reproach to a fool. . .

The red light of sunset was streaming into the entrance when we came forth after a sojourn of nearly two hours in the bowels of the mountain. . . Those who merely walk through, content with a hasty glance will find little to impede their movements. There is nothing to deter a woman, only she must leave her hoop at home, wear thick boots and make provision for looping up her skirts. Many an English lady would then enjoy a visit to Ingleborough Cave.

In his *Rambles by the Ribble*, Dobson agreed with Walter White; but his English ladies, with one lively exception, were not so sure about enjoying the stooping and creeping:

I must remark that our exploring party was a somewhat merry one. . . When we came to that part of the cave where Mr White tells us a thing is put into one's hand 'which you might take to be a scrubbing brush' the ladies of the party, with one exception, stopped short. They did not relish the stooping and the creeping – rather awkward for crinolin wearers:– one lady however, and young, pretty and spirited she was, was nothing daunted; with the patten in her right hand and the candle in her left, she crept through the narrow gulley and went to the far end of the cave along with the more adventurous members of the rougher sex.

Caves, Pot Holes and Limestone Pavements

The first time anyone explores a cave, they can hardly help asking themselves, or someone else, how and when this strange phenomenon, a great hole through the rock, was formed. The question tends to remain unanswered, partly because the process is very complicated; and even if an answer is forthcoming, it is very difficult to follow and understand. However, a simplified explanation must be attempted, since caves are such a remarkable feature of the Three Peaks landscape.

Caves in limestone have been formed by water; so much is simple. Rainwater, as it falls through the air, collects a tiny amount of carbon dioxide; then as it seeps through the earth it falls on, it collects even more. This mixture of H_2O and CO_2 (i.e. rainwater plus carbon dioxide) forms H_2CO_3. This is carbonic acid, which works on the limestone and dissolves it to form calcium bicarbonate; thus the diluted carbonic acid, dissolving the limestone along cracks and joints, forms a pattern of grykes (fissures) and clints (paving stones). The chemical equation looks like this:

$$H_2CO_3 \quad + \quad CaCO_3 \quad = \quad Ca(HCO_3)_2$$

Carbonic acid   Limestone   Calcium bicarbonate

Calcium bicarbonate is easily soluble in water; it collects and begins to seep along the tiny cracks and joints, gradually making them wider.

This process heralds the beginning of water pouring along ducts inside the limestone. Later, as the ducts get bigger, erosion by friction begins also to operate, as shales and grit are carried along the ducts, rubbing away the limestone as they pass.

But the process described above would never have taken place if the limestone in question had remained where it was formed, underneath the sea. Below sea level limestone doesn't let water through. So the process started only when earthquakes pushed the limestone up above sea level, and in doing this opened up those cracks or joints which served as one set of passages into which rainwater could flow. Another means of entry for water was offered by the natural pores in the limestone – that is, through the tiny spaces between the grains of which limestone is formed. And a third passage for water was offered by the layers

of silt or mud which are found in limestone, where such
sediments have bedded down over a period between two much
longer periods when the limestone was being formed by the
pressed-down layers of dead sea animals and coral. Along these
bedding planes the waters inside the limestone flowed and
escaped into the valleys.

The raising of the limestone above sea level is thought to have
taken place 30 million years ago; 29 million years later a series of
ice ages began. Glaciers formed, so that all but the very tops of
the Three Peaks was a sea of ice.

Glaciers started scraping away the sides of valleys, melted,
pushing mud and melting ice down into the passages in the
limestone; further melting sent waters down these passages,
washing the debris along and eroding the sides still more.
Further icing took place, further erosion of the valley sides and

valley bottoms. More passages inside the limestone were formed, and new passages gouged out for the waters to move through and out into the valleys. Naturally the waters found their own level, travelling along the deeper passages; and this means that some of the passages higher up in the limestone were no longer needed to carry water, and hence dry caves resulted where water would only flow after particularly heavy rainfall, a process we recognise in many of the normally dry caves which people explore today. This explains, of course, the dry entry to Ingleborough Cave, and the outlet now offered for the water lower down at Beck Head.

It is these processes which have shaped the distinctive landscape above ground, so vividly described a century ago by John Ruskin, in a comparison with the Jura Mountains:

> The first tracts of Jura differ in many ways from the limestone levels around Ingleborough. . .
> The Yorkshire moors are mostly by a hundred or two feet higher, and exposed to drifts of rain under violent and nearly constant wind. They break into wide fields of loose blocks and rugged slopes of shale, and are mixed with sands and clay from the millstone grit, which nourish rank grass and lodge in an occasional morass; the wild winds also forbidding any vestige or comfort of tree, except here and there in a sheltered nook of new plantation.
> A still greater and stranger difference exists in the system of streams. For all their losing themselves and hiding and intermitting, their presence is distinctly felt on a Yorkshire moor; one sees the place where they have been in yesterday, the wells where they will flow after the next shower, and a tricklet here at the bottom of a crag, or a tinkle there from the top of it, is always making one think whether this is one of the sources of the Aire or rootlets of the Ribble or beginnings of Bolton Strid, or threads of silver which are to be spun into the Tees. (*Praeterita*, 1885-9)

Further and more detailed information about Cave Formation can be acquired from Brian Paul Hindle's short pamphlet of that name, available from the Dales National Park Information Centres; also the *Guide to Ingleborough Cave and Gaping Gill* by Trevor Ford, available at the cave shop at Ingleborough Cave, has a useful and more detailed explanation of that cave than has been given above.

100

On reaching the entrance to Ingleborough Cave, or emerging from it, it is well worth continuing just a little further up the path, for it is less than half a mile to Trow Gill, the deep cutting through limestone cliffs which leads up to Gaping Gill. Passing over the ornamental bridge built by the Farrer brothers, which spans the water issuing from Beck Head, the path gets rougher. It lies between two slopes. In the more wooded slope on the left is to be found Dead Man's Cave where, in 1946, the clothed skeleton of a man was found; rumour has it that it was the body of an enemy agent dropped by parachute during the war, who lost his way and sought shelter in the cave.

756715   Further on still, and just before the path turns up towards Trow Gill, there is a wood spreading up the bank. At the corner of the wood is another cave, Foxholes, which also must once have given shelter, but to a much older example of homo sapiens, for here Neolithic implements were once found, and pieces of broken pottery – but no skeletons.

755716   Below the wood the path is barred by a gate and from here the canyon of Trow Gill comes into view. This, for some, might be the moment to admire, to take a photograph and turn back along the same route. The now familiar path leads agreeably downhill past the great cave, through the woods and down into the village. For those who hate to return by exactly the same way as they came, but who want to get back to Clapham, there are two other routes to choose from. The first begins by following the path past the cave and along the stream, but before reaching the little iron kissing gate at the entrance to the plantations, and just beyond the little hut containing the

753708   rhythmically audible ram pump, a rough path leads up the slope on the right to Clapdale Farm; today the farm belongs to the University of Lancaster and is used for caving parties and other outdoor studies and pursuits. There is a way through the farmyard leading to a track that skirts the top side of the wood. This is the track that Walter White had to walk up in 1850 because the untidy picnickers had caused the pleasanter Clapdale Drive to be closed to the public. It leads on down to the start of the drive.

There is a second rather different way back to the village by a track which leads along the other side of the valley, and from which there are some fine views. The track is called Long Lane, and it is not only long, it is very straight and fairly heavy going, even though it slopes downhill all the way. It is reached by

Trow Gill

756716
757717

passing through that gate from which such a good view up Trow Gill is to be had, and immediately turning off right, up a steep ravine beside a wall. Near the top there is a gate in the wall on the right which is the entrance to Long Lane, the bridleway to Clapham, bounded on each side by walls or the ruins of walls. At the start of the slope down there is a magnificent aerial view of Trow Gill on the right, and some way further on, looking left, one may get a glimpse of the famous Norber Boulders on the skyline. These are 'erratics', that is they don't 'belong' where they are, but were carried up the slope from half a mile away by the last glacier to make its way, slower than a snail, across this landscape. The boulders of Silurian rock were deposited on top of the limestone surface of Norber as the glacier melted. The surface limestone, being softer than the rocks out of which the boulders are made, has been eroded by rain and has therefore sunk, except of course where the surface was sheltered from the rain by the boulder. This has had the effect of leaving the dark grey boulders balancing on small plinths of white limestone, looking as though they had been put there by a very powerful fork-lift truck, ready for a geological exhibition. But a fuller explanation of this whole process is given below, on page 105.

752695

Long Lane joins Thwaite Lane at right angles just before the village. To the right are the tunnels leading back to the village under the grounds of Ingleborough Hall. To the left Thwaite Lane, which is part of an old pack-horse route from Lancaster to Richmond, leads to Austwick. Anyone wishing to visit those Norber Boulders (and they are well worth a visit) is recommended to make a diversion and go this way. A little

760692

more than half a mile along Thwaite Lane there is a ladder stile beside a gate on the left, with a signpost to Norber. Before the stile there are two things worth noticing; the first is Robin Procter's Scar that rises impressively on the left. It got its name from a wretched local farmer who lost his way, riding home from a pub one night, and went over the top, losing his life but preserving his name. The second point of interest is the little hump in the roadway just before reaching the ladder stile. This is not, as one might think, a misplaced sleeping policeman such as one finds across roads to slow down traffic, but a low tunnel under the road to allow sheep to pass from the field on one side of the track to the field on the other side. A strange piece of civil engineering, inspired no doubt, if not constructed, by one of the

Farrer family who – as we have seen – had a penchant for tunnels.

On the other side of the stile the path leads diagonally across a wide field, passing on the left a tumbledown wall which completely encircles a round expanse of reedy grass. Local farmers say it was once a tarn which was drained, leaving a treacherous marsh – hence the need for a wall to keep the sheep from sinking in. But even the marsh has now dried off so that it offers no hazard to sheep or shepherd.

Another stile takes the path under the lea of the scar, and some of the Norber Boulders, dark grey against the whiter limestone, begin to appear. A path strikes off left up the slope, and leads onto the Norber plateau where it is worth spending a little time wandering around these strange misplaced rocks, some of which have been split neatly into two pieces by the

763695

action of ice, or by a cheeky tree putting its roots into a fissure, or even, it is reported, by some student geologists from London (it *would* be London!) who went at one of the rocks with a sledge hammer. One can only echo the remark of Walter White's guide quoted on page 90.

At the end of the scar a signpost points straight ahead to Crummack, to the right to Austwick and, of course, back to Clapham. The view across to Moughton (pronounced *mooton*) and along the valley of the Wenning towards Horton is immensely impressive. It was from Crummack Dale and the sides of Moughton that the Boulders are thought to have been transported. The process is vividly described by David Crutchley in his *Geology of the Three Peaks*, where he writes of the Norber Boulders as some of the best examples of glacial erratics to be found in Britain.

> Their story starts in the Ice Age. The valley glacier which once occupied Crummackdale eroded down into the older Silurian and Ordovician rocks below the Great Scar Limestone beds. The process of erosion in operation at the base of the valley glacier enabled the moving ice actually to pluck large blocks of rock from the valley floor. These were transported within the moving ice mass. . . At the mouth of Crummackdale the valley glacier turned right into the main flow of ice, and it was forced to climb up and over the shoulder of Norber Brow. At the end of the Ice Age . . . the glacier melted and deposited the large blocks of Silurian rock on the ice scarred limestone of Norber Brow. The result is that a young rock, the limestone, is now underneath a relatively older rock, the Silurian blocks. . . The Silurian blocks have protected the limestone immediately under them from all the various processes of erosion that have been active since the end of the Ice Age. . . Consequently some of the blocks are perched on pedestals of limestone. . .

Norber boulder

752727

But this has been a long diversion, which began at the lower end of Trow Gill. For those wanting to make for Ribblehead there are again two possible routes, one through Trow Gill up to Gaping Gill and then across the marshy moorland to join Clapham Lane. The other is to get onto Clapham Lane by the short route already described for those who wanted to return to Clapham via Long Lane, for Long Lane becomes Clapham Lane just above Trow Gill.

Gaping Gill is not much more than a mile away from the bottom of Trow Gill, but the path rises steadily. There are two explanations as to how Trow Gill, now a dry valley, was formed. It used to be said that it was once a long cave that has 'caved in'; however, it is now thought to have been eroded by the waters of the melting glaciers. From the top of Trow Gill the path passes a stile on the left that can be disregarded; a second stile on the left leads over the wall to Bar Pot. This is a wide and deep hole with a cave at the bottom down which really experienced cavers travel, suitably protected with wet suits and crash helmets, nylon rope ladders and acetylene headlamps to get into the main chamber of Gaping Gill. The surface path to Gaping Gill crosses some limestone pavement before reaching the perimeter fence of Gaping Gill itself. The hole is 365 feet deep (an easy statistic to remember), and when it has been raining hard for a long time, the waterfall pouring into it from Fell Beck will be twice the height of Niagara. Normally the water falling into the hole is no more than a trickle. When it gets to the gravelly lower basement of the hole it sinks through the surface to appear again, about a mile away, at Beck Head next to Ingleborough Cave.

Gaping Gill was first successfully descended by a Frenchman called Martel, who used rope ladders, and the help of his wife. He accomplished the feat on 1 August 1895, taking only twenty-three minutes to reach the bottom. He kept in touch with Madame Martel at the top by telephone. A full description of the expedition is given in *Yorkshire Caves and Potholes* by A. Mitchell (Dalesman, 1949). Today, inexperienced potholers can get down in 90 seconds, in a bosun's chair. This is operated by local caving clubs on the spring and summer bank holiday weekends with a winch. Inflation makes any mention of price unrealistic and obsolescent, but probably one can reckon it will cost at least as much as four pints of beer, whatever they may be worth at the time of descent. (There is a heavy joke that they let you down free; the charge is for pulling you up.)

There is a well worn path up to the top of Ingleborough from Gaping Gill, and many will want to make for it. But our goal is Ribblehead and, unless it is misty, it is worth aiming for 758730 Clapham Lane by striking out north-eastwards to Marble Pot. This demands good map-reading, and a compass would prove 762729 useful; beyond Marble Pot is Jockey Hole, and from here a path leads north along a line of potholes until the track from Horton 765739 to the top of Ingleborough comes into view. To the right this track crosses Clapham Lane after less than a mile before reaching 777735 Sulber Nick on the way to Horton. But the route to Ribblehead via Selside leads off northwards at this crossing, that is to the left, and this part of the walk is included in the second route, which follows.

757716

Starting again at the bottom of Trow Gill the first short lap will be the same as that leading to the gate at the start of Long Lane which has been described on page 103. Do not, however, turn right down Long Lane. Instead, take the path that starts off leftwards, i.e. northwards, almost immediately bearing right, then swinging left, skirting a dip in the moor known as Clapham Bottoms. There is then about a mile of pleasant walking along the grassy track. This is Clapham Lane which most of the time keeps to the same contour. Then the grass on the left gradually gets taken over by a bank of limestone pavements, while on the right a wall comes up from a slope to turn and follow the path, which gradually gets narrower. A look over the other side of the wall reveals a quite remarkable scene. A long way below, a frozen sea of limestone pavement, Thwaite Scars, stretches away into the distance. Where the wall on the right comes to an end there is a gate, and from the other side of the gate an even more impressive view of the pavements opens up. They stretch away towards the green pastures of Crummock Dale on the right, while that scarred expanse of pavement descending in huge precipice steps streaks away to the front.

These strange scars on the limestone landscape need an explanation all to themselves, for they are a special feature of the landscape on both sides of upper Ribblesdale. When the surface of this Great Scar Limestone, as we see it now, was being formed under the sea, it was of course as flat as a sandy shore; and under this surface was a solid bed, sometimes 300 feet thick, of similar limestone, since it was all made of the shells of fish and corals which had lived and died in the warm tropical sea covering the surface of the globe at this spot. Earthquakes moved it upwards out of the water, so the sea retreated and cracks appeared as a result. The surface became covered with silt and grits brought down by rivers. The next stage was the appearance of glaciers which stripped much of the surface bare. Rain fell on it, entering the cracks and splits in the surface, cutting the grykes and leaving the clints, as described on page 137. The process continued over hundreds of years. The deeper grykes have proved hospitable seed-beds for various flowers and ferns, some of them pretty common such as Hart's Tongue, whose shiny feather-shaped green leaves push up to find the light. Herb Robert is common too; less common is the Rock Rose. In some grykes wild raspberries (with rather small fruits) and honeysuckle abound, and in July the bright vermilion flowers of Bloody Cranesbill shine out against the white stone.

Leaving this singular landscape the path continues northwards, keeping to a raised shelf of limestone from which Penyghent is seen over to the right, lying like a long and comfortable sphinx on the other side of the valley. The track tends to wither away, but soon a ladder stile indicates the right of way and, diagonally crossing a field to another ladder, the path leads to a green lane walled on each side which after a couple of hundred yards comes to a T-junction. To the left over a stile lies Alum Pot, and to the right down a rocky rutted road, the little hamlet of Selside.

789756

775756

Anyone intending to visit Alum Pot should go first down the lane to Selside Farm (between the main road and the railway) in order to get a permit (since Alum Pot is in a pasture belonging to the farm). Alternatively one can get a permit from the Old Reading Room on the road. But the little hamlet of Selside has at least two houses worth attention, besides the Old Reading Room. There was once a little school here and a pub called the Red Lion. With few exceptions all the buildings are of a piece; even the Shaws, which was obviously 'improved' in the 18th century, stems clearly from the same Dales stock. The exception is the modern bungalow built by, and belonging to, Leeds University Union, which is planted unobtrusively among the trees to the north of the track.

Vernacular Buildings

Raistrick, in his *Pennine Dales*, 1968, gives a fine and true impression of traditional Dales buildings, his dry North Country style matching admirably the architecture he describes:

> The sheer hard practicality of house and farm buildings, of bridges, churches and schools robs them of the chance to display ornament or to give play to architectural fancy. A solidity in unity and balance with a natural environment gives an air of fitness and stability, and imparts character to many modest buildings which would be of no note in a richer context and a kinder climate.

Although monastic records, rent rolls and parish registers make it clear that most of the farms around the Three Peaks date back far into the past, the majority of the farmhouse buildings in the area were put up between 1650 and 1750. For the most part they are long and low, having low ceilings and only one storey above the ground floor, and often with a 'laithe' (or barn) or a 'shippon' (cowshed) built on as part of the house at one end, or even both. The walls consist of 'rubble', that is undressed limestone, such as has always been used for dry-stone walls. For building houses, however, plenty of mortar had to be used, both to hold the stones together and to face the outside so that no draughts or rainwater should come through. Lime for the mortar, of course, presented no problem here, being easily made in the kilns by burning the ubiquitous limestone. Roofs were originally of stone slabs found in the Yoredale Series and extensively quarried in the area. Welsh or Lake District slates and even asbestos tiles have today sometimes replaced these, but they are still in position on many local buildings. The stone 'slates' were very large, thick and heavy, so good timber, often oak, was necessary for the roof beams, and their considerable weight demanded an exceptionally low pitch to the roof, so that they would not slip downwards. The largest slabs, often as much as a yard square, were set on the lowest course and resting on the supporting wall. The size of the slabs diminished as the tiler moved up towards the ridge of the roof. Each tile was attached to the purlins by a large nail driven through a hole pierced at the top of the slab.

The floors of the ground-floor rooms were of huge square flags; if they are green they came from the Ingleton quarries, and if blue, from those at Horton. Horton Flags, quarried at Helwith Bridge or Arco Wood nearby, were used also for broad shelves in the dairy or pantry, for the sides of water-butts and for 'boskins', dividing the stalls in the 'shippon' where the cattle were kept. In the quarries around Helwith Bridge, and especially at Arco Wood, now disused but listed as a geological site of national importance, the Horton Flags can be seen *in situ*, layer against layer of Silurian rock, standing on end against the hillside, 'with massive beds of limestone lying in horizontal layers across the upturned edges' (Raistrick: *The Pennine Dales*).

It is not surprising then that the walls of the buildings near these quarries are exceptional. No need to use limestone rubble here, for the thick smooth Silurian slates were to hand and easy to lay one on top of the other, and required less mortar. The farmhouse and buildings at Studfold, north of the road between Helwith Bridge and Horton, is a good example of this. In the typical vernacular buildings hereabouts windows were usually small and mullioned. The front door often led directly into the

Penyghent viewed from Selside

main room, known as the houseplace, and having generally a porch jutting out, roofed by two great Horton slates set against each other at an angle. The farmhouses were often isolated, strung out along a hillside on the contour where the springs emerged. Although a barn or cowshed might be attached directly to one end of the farmhouse, many small, isolated barns are to be found in the pastures. Often these have been built on the sloping sides of the valley, with one opening onto the pasture at the higher side so that wagons could be driven in, or the hay brought in easily, and another opening on the lower side where the cattle would be driven into their stalls for milking, or for shelter in winter. But because of the slope, what was the ground floor where the hay was stored was also the upper floor as far as the cow stalls were concerned, and so the hay could be shot down to the feeding troughs with a minimum expenditure of energy. There would be room in these isolated barns for about eight to sixteen beasts. Here the cows would be milked, morning and evening, without having to be driven far over the fields. The milk used to be carried back to the dairy at the farmhouse in back-cans, which held from six to eight gallons and looked rather like the cans continental *vignerons* carry attached to their backs when they spray their vines.

Frog-prince in Colt Park Wood

Now back to Selside. At the end of the lane leading from Alum Pot, and on a corner a few yards up the Settle-Ribblehead road, lies Top Farm, skewed at an angle to the road in order to face the midday sun, characteristic evidence of good sense and an example followed by many of the houses along the Settle road, and indeed elsewhere. Top Farm is a typical long Dales house, having the laithe built directly onto the main house at the east end. Two sets of small mullioned windows are on the left of the front door, no doubt the original windows, if not the original glass. They may not let much light into the rooms inside, but they don't let out much heat, or let in much cold, and this was always a more important consideration than light in this climate.

The porch over the front door has an inscription on the lintel: **I * H 1726**, but the house itself may well be older.

The other large house in Selside is the Shaws. It is faced with squared blocks of limestone and sandstone and has a stone roof. The porch is very elegant, with fluted Ionic pilasters, above which is inscribed **J – J 1738**. But the door itself is a design of some 50 years earlier than the porch, evidence that the house was once 'improved'.

The main road from Selside to Ribblehead makes a dull walk, 778756 so a visit to Alum Pot and then a walk back through the fields is recommended, even though this does involve a short stretch of the dull road. The clump of trees surrounding the great pothole somehow takes away the horror or fear one might feel on looking down the sheer 250 feet to the bottom, which in fact can hardly be seen, and can be viewed with relative safety from only a small number of places around the perimeter. Half way down the wide shaft, in the north wall, is a passage entrance, or exit, as may be, through which one may sometimes see cavers emerging who have followed the passage underground from 774756 Diccan Pot, about 200 yards across the field to the north-west. But the passage is perilous and should *not* be undertaken without an expert in charge. The water which can be heard roaring just inside the entrance to Diccan Cave is rushing down to fall into Alum Pot, there joining the waters of Alum Pot Beck which falls into the great hole from the south-west rim. The combined streams flow from the bottom of the cave, not into the Ribble half a mile away (as one might expect), but into a small tarn called Turn Dub on the other side of the Ribble, having passed underground, under the river itself.

Professor Boyd Dawkins, Professor of Geology at Manchester University, wrote in his *Cave Hunting*, 1874, that the first known descent of Alum Pot (known then as Helln Pot) was made in 1848. Boyd Dawkins himself made what he claimed was the third descent in the spring of 1870.

> The apparatus employed consisted of a windlass supported on two baulks of timber and a bucket covered with a shield, sufficiently large to hold two people, and two guiding ropes to prevent the rotation of the bucket in mid-air.
>
> A party of navvies were employed to look after the mechanical contrivances, and two ladders about 8 feet long were in readiness in case they should be needed. Thirteen of us went down including three ladies. . . We arrived at the top after about five hours work, wet to the skin.

But for those looking for a cave experience which is quite safe, a short walk over the fields from Alum Pot to Borrins Moor Cave is recommended. The entrance to it is not easy to find, being obstructed by a large boulder, and sunk in one of the many hollows in the reedy moorland. It is best approached over the stile due east of Alum Pot. After the stile, one needs to turn half left over or between the boulders and then over the marshy grass.

It is worth exploring a number of the hollows which might contain the cave entrance before finding it, and it is important to take a good torch. After climbing over the boulder which bars the entrance, the amateur caver is confronted with a long, usually dry passage, high enough not to need a helmet and level enough not to need much exertion, which leads 250 yards under the moor. Going then becomes uncomfortable and, later, dangerous, so those with more discretion than valour should turn back.

There is no right of way over the fields directly to the north to Ribblehead, but for anyone wanting to look at the remains of a 774759 Romano–British colony, 500 yards away the mounds and outlines of walls below Whit-a-Green Rocks are clearly to be seen. There is a path up from Alum Pot Lane past the Leeds University Union bungalow mentioned above, and the disturbed surface of the field can be seen between the spring half way up the field and the wall at the end of it.

In making for Ribblehead it is worth taking the road from Selside for nearly half a mile, and then turning off left at the fifth 783763 gate, to go diagonally over the field.

114

This is an ancient right of way. It was already established and designated on the 'Enclosure Map', dated 1791, which can be examined at the headquarters of the Yorkshire Archeological Society's offices in Leeds. This indicates which of the fields were to be enclosed, and how they would be allocated to particular named farmers. The walls enclosing the fields still stand today, and the footpath referred to above is clearly marked as beginning in the fourth field along from Alum Pot Lane and labelled: 'Footpath to Cold [sic] Park'. Today the path is not clearly marked on the ground, but after walking up the slope from the road for about 20 yards, one can see a ladder stile on the other side of the field, indicating that the right of way still stands. From the top of this stile a second can be seen at the far side of the next field. At the top corner of the third field, where the trees of Colt Park Wood begin to thin out, a short snicket passes through a narrow neck of the wood, shut off at the nearer end by a wicket gate and protected by a stile at the upper end. A notice board inside the wood and beside the path announces that the wood is a National Nature Reserve and permission to enter the wood should be obtained in advance from the Regional Office, 33 Eskdale Terrace, Newcastle upon Tyne NE2 4DN.

774770

hernside from the south

J.E. Lousley, in his *Wild Flowers of Chalk and Limestone*, 1950, calls it 'one of the most remarkable and uncanny woods in Britain'. On pages 186-7 he gives what he calls a brief account of the wood. Certainly for those with specialist botanical knowledge and a good camera it offers richness, but for them or anyone else who ventures into the wood it presents also serious risks of a broken leg, for the grykes are often treacherously concealed by grass and foliage. They are wide, irregularly spaced, and often several yards deep. The right of way is, as usual, indicated by the ladder stile over the first wall, about 100 yards from the edge of the wood.

The main reason why the wood harbours rare plants is that no cows or sheep have ever been able to graze there; at least the dead body of an occasional trespassing sheep is evidence of the fate that awaits them if they do. This has meant that plants which might have been eaten by livestock have survived. In particular, trees have been able to grow to a fair height. Rabbits enjoy life here and they are of course a threat to young trees, for they like the bark. However those that grow to any height are

Limestone pavements

less tasty, and at least they don't get rubbed bare by scratching sheep or cattle. Ash predominates, along with bird cherry, whose short-lived blossom gives off a lovely scent in early summer, and which provides a growing place for the ugly and nastily-named fungus Jew's Ear, which normally prefers elderberry to grow upon. Another reason why rare plants flourish here is that the micro-climate in the deep grykes offers a home which is relatively undisturbed, sheltered from winds and where the soil is especially acid, as favoured by many ferns: Hart's Tongue, Maidenhair, Spleenwort and a variety of other ferns and mosses of interest to experts. As for flowers, Herb Robert abounds: better to call it by its country name, Stinking Jenny, as a reminder that such a delicate, pretty plant can be so repellant. Much more rare is Herb Paris – having always two 'pairs' of leaves, which suggested no doubt another name for it, True Love. The name has nothing to do with the capital of France. William Turner wrote of it that: 'It hath four leaves lyke unto a great plantaine, and in the overmost top a little blacke bery lyke a blacke morberry but blacker and greater.' A third herb evidently to be found in the wood is Herb Christopher, or Baneberry, the latter name indicating that the berry is deadly poisonous, a fact obviously recognised in Germany, where it is called *Teufelsbeere* (Devil's Berry), and in France where it is the Devil's Grape, *Raisin du Diable*. The association with St Christopher is less obvious but may be because the rootlets, if sectioned, reveal a cross or a star.

At the end of the wood on the left is a fine proud barn, high and long, a good example of the economic system described above (see page 112), where the hay can be unloaded, in this case from a wagon entering through the high porch on the upper side, and then in winter fed through a trap door in the floor to the cattle which have their stalls on the lower floor. This, of course, for them (entering on the side opposite where the hay is brought in and unloaded), is the ground floor.

773779   Colt Park farmhouse lies ahead. The building is little more than a hundred years old, but one indication that there has been an inhabited house here for much longer than that is the date-stone lintel on the west side of the house, which must have come from an earlier building. It is inscribed **1663 T H**, which refers almost certainly to the 'Thomas Howson of Coltparke' to be found, so written, in the Ingleton parish register as having been buried 'in woollen in the north quire' on 1 January 1679.

The track to the right from Colt Park leads through large limestone rocks surmounted by rowan trees and mountain ash. Here, in August and September, the grass between the trees and rocks is bedecked with harebells. Can it be that the sheep which often graze here and keep the grass short don't relish harebells? If so, this is a blessing.

Anyone going down this track and looking over the wall into the wood will, at the end of the summer, be treated to the sight of a huge crop of Giant Bell Flowers, standing proudly erect and towering over the ferns and nettles.

774785

Before the bridge over the railway there is a fine example of an old limekiln on the left of the track, and just beyond the cattle grid is the disused Salt Lake quarry. A notice the far side of the wall tells passers-by that entry is prohibited without a permit. The quarry is protected by the Yorkshire Naturalists' Trust (20 Castlegate, York YO1 1RP) and belongs to British Rail. Permits can be obtained from the Trust, and membership forms too. The quarry is a charming little 'reserve', sheep and cattle being excluded, since the passing trains and the sheer cliff faces would be a constant threat for them. Stagnant pools and, in rainy weather, several waterfalls tumbling down the cliff face favour the flowers, and the growth of tufa (see page 29). Viper's Bugloss grows in the mounds of gravel, and up on the ledge Coral Root Orchid has been found, and photographed – in fact the warden once found a large lady doing just this, lying on her front. Unfortunately she was also lying on three Coral Root Orchids growing there! A common and (I think) very attractive feature are the bullrushes which stick up from the stagnant pools. Unfortunately, in spite of the notice, they sometimes disappear when in full flower, only, I suppose, to stand unsuitably in some chilly fireplace, possibly dyed blue or red. Once again, I can't help echoing Walter White's guide (see page 90). I seem to have mentioned only summer and autumn flowers. But towards the end of May, Bird's Eye Primrose, Ladies' Mantle and Sweet Cicely have been found and photographed in the quarry. Just over the railway bridge stands the row of six Salt Lake Cottages. They were built by the Midland Railway for their linesmen and signalmen more than 100 years ago; they have a strangely urban look about them, with their steep slate roofs and separate little washhouses and

775785
765793

coal stores. After the last cottage the track joins the main road which leads to the left to the green triangle of Ribblehead.

19 July

Four days of continuous summer rain; then I woke to a clear blue sky. It was a noisy morning. The stream, of course, was flood-full and the wind in the chestnut and beech trees was whirling great waves of sound round the house. It was just after six. I checked at the window that I'd not been deceived, pulled on clothes and went out into the yard. A great volume of vintage air filled my head and chest. I'd do something useful; collect peat from the hilltop to put on the celery. I folded a black plastic refuse bag into my pocket, found a short broken spade and started up.

The sun was over the wood by the time I set off, shining horizontally across the drumlins which showed up proudly as if they were full of air, great brown eliptical bubbles lying on the valley bottom. In the distance the lambs were crying for their mothers. The higher I went the stronger the wind, roaring down the mountain. I turned my back on it and looked back at the view: an excuse to get my breath back.

The cows in the pastures were gathered around pools and serpenting streams of *gold*; the early sun was bouncing off the water into my eyes. I went on up through the reedy grass, quite long now, with scabious pushing its way up alongside bedraggled buttercups, but no sign of Grass of Parnassus yet. Too early. The hill got very steep; I followed a recently cut drain. Water poured down it continuously over clay, then shale, then pebbles; it was real pure clay. I scooped some out and made a cricket ball with it! The grass was shorter here. Little yellow four-petalled stars shone out from the tangled turf. I remembered the name: tormentil. It's sometimes called 'bloodrot'; reputedly the little red roots boiled up in milk would cure the torments – i.e. the colic. Later there was a little patch of

harebells balancing beautifully on their delicate stems. In Devon they're called Ding Dongs! And then, on a patch of bright green grass, those little brown mushrooms with tall very thin stems. I pocketed a couple of dozen.

Across the valley Whernside was lit up. Yesterday its great green flank was striped with vertical white watercourses; now the stripes were black grooves where the water had washed the grass away and dug deep into the hill. The slope flattened out. Over the other side of the wall the great peat field started, a wide expanse of peat bunkers between great, flat, red-brown sheets of peat, good to walk across, like a firm foam-rubber carpet underfoot. Seeds of silver birch have been found in the peat on these tops, evidence of a birch forest once on this bare plateau. It must have looked magnificent.

I went over to the overhanging rims of peat, cut great chocolate chunks out of the sides and nearly filled my bag. It was a bit damp, so heavy. But the way down was steep; I could, with great effort, pull my bag after me, and it slid. In the old days – a hundred years ago – they would load the peat onto sledges which would have been pulled up, empty, by donkeys. Then a sledge-ride down the slopes over the rocks and ridges.

Sheep scattered as I approached, fleeing through a hole in the wall ahead. I slid down with my bag, coming to a stop at a stone. The wind was dropping. I watched a toy train, a line of trucks, trundle across the viaduct. Then a late curlew rose and circled, calling loudly. Was it a single parent looking after a second family? Up and off down again. As I reached the stile to get over the wall to sprinkle my peat on the celery, the damned bag split! But I rescued most of the peat and came happily back to breakfast – coffee and bacon and mushrooms, morning-gathered.

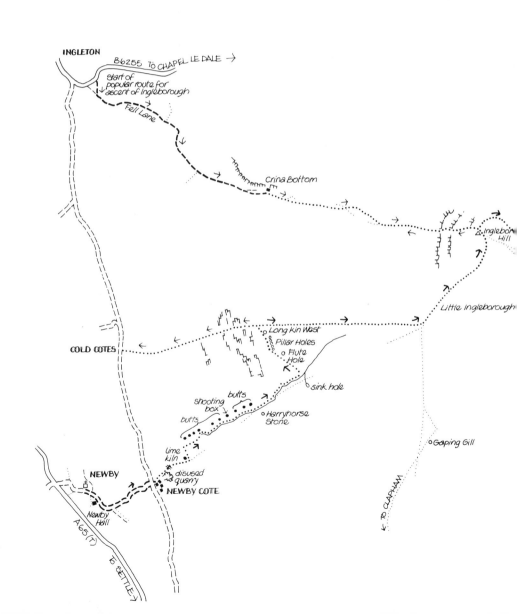

INGLETON

B6255 To CHAPEL LE DALE →

start of
popular route for
ascent of Ingleborough

Fell Lane

Crina Bottom

Ingleborough
Hill

Little Ingleborough

Long kin West

Pillar Holes

Flute
Hole

sink hole

COLD COTES

butts

shooting
box

butts

Harryhorse
Stone

Gaping Gill

lime
kiln

disused
quarry

NEWBY

NEWBY COTE

Newby
Hall

A65 (T)

TO SETTLE

TO CLAPHAM

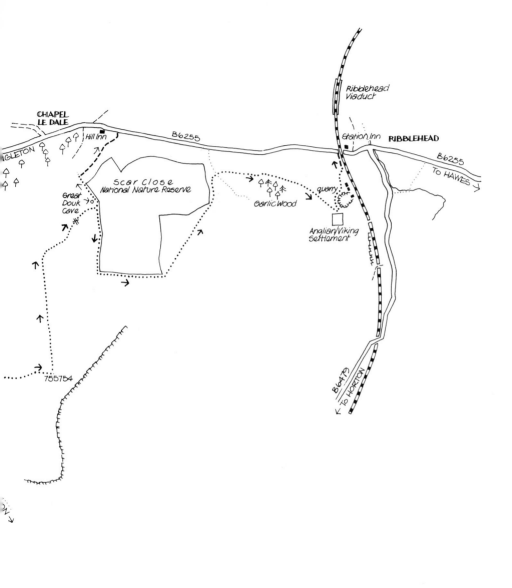

CHAPEL
LE DALE

Hill Inn

IGLETON

B6255

Scar Close
National Nature Reserve

Garlic Wood

Ribblehead
Viaduct

Station Inn RIBBLEHEAD

B6255

TO HAWES

quarry

Great
Douk
Cave

Anglian/Viking
Settlement

B6479
TO HORTON

755754

Ingleborough Hill

Chapter 4   From Newby up Ingleborough and down to Ribblehead

Ingleborough is a mountain of character, the king of Yorkshire heights, whose superiority is enhanced, not diminished, by being called Ingleborough Hill. There are few Yorkshire-born who don't know and respect it; many have climbed it; and they look back on the demanding experience as a duty proudly done. It's almost as compelling as the visit they make, once in a lifetime at least, to York Minister.

There are five or six well-worn ways up to the top, but I'll suggest a special one, where few fellow walkers will be met, even on a fine summer's day. I can also recommend doing this walk when the snow covers the peaks; the view of all three white against a clear blue sky (and they can all be taken in at a glance on the way up) is as breath-taking as the climb itself, which in fact isn't so very steep. Before my description of this less popular route, many will, all the same, want to know
702731   something of the most popular. This starts just outside Ingleton, opposite the last house, Storrs Hall, on the Hawes Road. The path leads across Storrs Common onto Fell Lane, a green road between two walls. On the left, at the start of the lane, are mounds and embankments. One of these used to carry the little narrow-gauge railway from the quarries near Whitescar Cave round to the main line; but neither track has survived. The mounds are the remains of shooting butts. These were not made for sportsmen, but for the BEF (British Expeditionary Force) in 1914. Here farmers' boys and miners' sons practised rifle shooting before going off to Flanders – a sad reminder of another age.

Fell Lane leads up to the attractive, well-sheltered and isolated
723736   little farm called Crina Bottom, and from then on the path gradually becomes steeper; as it gets nearer to the top, great

angular boulders lie scattered around as if they had been left there by playful giants after a fight. Many are composed of sealed-together slabs of slate, like solid puff pastry; sliced across they would make huge paving stones or unbelievably heavy roof tiles. Higher up still the slabs become thinner, and the well-worn path which now becomes more a stairway in stone is marked by untidy cairns. And then suddenly a great pile of stones announces the top. But the top of Ingleborough demands a proper survey which can wait till after the description of the recommended and less well-trodden route which starts from the little village of Newby, between Clapham and Ingleton.

742746

Newby is a surprising little village. Cottages surround the village green, some very old, with small windows and their original roofs of thick local 'slates', some respectable Victorian and others very recent and no doubt conforming, but in a most ugly way, to the regulations as to appearance stipulated by the Craven District Council Planning Committee. One can easily picture the breeze blocks behind those neatly cemented local stones which decorate the outer faces of these intruders. There is a little 19th-century chapel; a rather arrogant 'thirties village school (now closed for want of children) with tall windows; and a fine but modest old manor house, tucked away from the building line beside some old cottages. The doorway is surmounted by a lintel containing two arched panels, one with the date **1670** and the other with the initials **P I M**. The manor house, marked as Newby Hall on the os map, stands on the site of a grange of Furness Abbey (for an explanation of granges see page 128). At the exit of the village, at the east end, there is another rather fine house with a first-floor room extending over the porch, which has a sundial above it carved in stone. But Newby has no shop, no post office, no pub and no church.

733706

The road which leads up through the village from the relatively new A65 (which runs from Settle to Kendal) joins the old road from Ingleton to Clapham, and just beyond the junction on the old road is the little hamlet of Newby Cote, which also is a former grange of Furness Abbey.

Monasteries and Granges

It is probably worth digressing here to wonder about these Abbey lands. The three Abbeys owning land on and around the Three Peaks area were Cistercian, maintaining their original connection with the parent monastery at Citeaux in Burgundy.

Fountains, near Ripon, owned parts of the slopes of Penyghent; Jervaulx near Masham, parts of upper Ribblesdale including Horton and Studfold; while Furness, not far from Barrow, north of Morecambe Bay, was the biggest landowner in the area, their properties stretching from Selside up to Gearstones, including granges at Ingman Lodge and Colt Park. They also took over former Norse settlements along the southern flank of Whernside, establishing granges at Bruntscar and Birkwith, as well as on the south side of Ingleborough at Newby and Newby Cote.

The Cistercians, more than any other religious order, developed this system of granges; unlike others they were not content to live off the rents of valuable properties left to them, nor did they go in for missionary work; their aim was to withdraw as much as possible from the world, and so they tried as far as possible to be self-sufficient in food and clothing. This they achieved by developing and improving their lands, particularly, in this area, for raising sheep.

At first they concentrated on the land close to their own monasteries, but opportunities to expand and take in adjoining land were limited in the more inhabited parts. It was doubtless for this reason that they started to acquire property on 'unencumbered lands', on the margin of existing settlements. It was on these primarily

> that their zeal and their genius would be lavished, and in the creation of that characteristically Cistercian institution, the independent monastic grange. They did this by establishing a series of easily managed units, worked by a team of lay brothers who were assigned there by the monastery, under the general supervision of a visiting official known as the Cellarer, based at the abbey. (Colin Platt: *The Monastic Grange in Medieval England*, Macmillan, 1969)

Arthur Raistrick gives a picture of life on the granges (*The Pennine Dales*, 1968):

> There was a constant coming and going between grange and abbey . . . the Cellarer, Prior and other officials came at regular intervals to hold courts and check accounts and give some supervision of affairs. Wool, cheese, grain, building materials and other produce of the granges was carried to the abbey, and wine and food was sent out to the granges. . . The grange generally had a chapel, at which its workpeople and tenants could hear Mass. This and the refectory were in the charge of a priest–monk. . .

Raistrick goes on to point out that the lay brothers, under the supervision of the monks, were directly responsible for the clearing of the trees and scrub from the hills, for draining the swamps, and for the resulting improvement in both pastures and flocks.

But of all our three abbeys, Furness in particular seems an unlikely landlord for estates so far distant. As the crow flies, the Abbey is over 40 miles from Newby. But it must have required several days' walk to make the journey on foot (monks were seldom mounted) around the coast of Morecambe Bay and through Kendal to the slopes of Ingleborough. Sometimes, no doubt, a short cut could be made across Morecambe sands, but even today this is rather a risky crossing.

The Coucher Books of Furness Abbey, edited from the original by John Brownhill (Chetham Society, 1916) give evidence of various deals and lawsuits relating to the Abbey lands. There is interesting evidence here that the geographical disadvantage of Furness worked to the advantage of

unscrupulous Yorkshire neighbours of the monks' estates at Newby . . . for these could bring their suits at any time to local wapentake courts, and as the abbot could not always receive warning, or, if warned, might not be able to cross the sands, nor have time to go round the long way, he often lost his cases. Hence he was allowed to appoint special local attorneys to act for him.

Some of the extant depositions of the courts indicate one way in which the Abbey acquired lands:

Robert de Boivill, Margaret his wife and their sons give to the monks a moiety [half] of Newby. The monks gave six marks to Robert and a gold ring to his wife. (1170)

But more was to come out of this:

> Robert de Boivill confirmed to the abbey the moiety of
> Newby on condition that he, his wife and his sons should all
> have burial in the monks' cemetery. . .
>
> Waldegrave son of Edmund grants to the monks Newby
> near Clapham . . . with pasture rights from above Newby
> towards Ingleborough. (1165)
>
> Henry III confirms the gift of Newby to the Monks. (1270)

On April 1537 Henry VIII 'received' the abbey. The various
granges, taken from the monks of Furness

> remained fixed down to recent times, for subdivision was
> discouraged or prohibited, on account, it was said, of the
> need for having a substantial body of yeomen for the defence
> of the border against the Scots. (Platt: *op. cit.*)

But enough of the monks. Let's return to the twentieth
century and to the little farmstead of Newby Cote, the name
indicating its position on the side of Ingleborough, this being a
nice marriage of the Viking with more recent Norman French.

Norber

Newby Cote consists of four houses. It looks out over Lancashire, whose landscape contrasts strikingly with that of the Three Peaks; rolling dark green fields shaped by hedges compare strangely with the yellow-browns of the Dales, where the slopes and valley bottoms are cut into irregular patterns by the grey stone walls. The largest house of the hamlet dates from 1660, according to the lintel at the back of the house. Unfortunately the front is rendered with pebble dash. This is a not uncommon feature of the stone houses in the area and must have seemed to those who started the practice, probably about 100 years ago, a good way to keep the damp from penetrating the irregular stone walls. They were deceived, for all too often, after a number of years, the damp penetrates the mortar so that a film of damp clings to the outer wall, gradually seeping into the inside walls of the house. Better far to have pointed those stones fairly regularly.

Like the last house in Newby the front porch has a first storey which increases the size of the first-floor room above it. In the front, dripstones deflect the rain and prevent it dripping onto the glass. They span the whole length of the windows, dropping down at each end, and then extend an inch or two sideways. The lintel over the back door – which may well once have been over the door at the front – has two carved panels with the letters **CG** above and **IVLC** below. The other has **1660** carved above with **I H** below, initials standing for the name of the owner at the time of building.

A lane leads up from the road past the end of the house, skirting a disused quarry on the right. A ladder stile confirms that this is a Right of Way onto the moor. Over the wall on the left is an enclosure pasture, with the ruin of a limekiln inside the corner of the wall as it strikes off west along the hillside. The path follows the wall westwards. But after only about 50 yards, to the right of the path, a delapidated (literally!) stone shooting butt with a sunken stone floor pushes its way up from the grass. This is the moment to turn off the path and strike up the slope beside the butt. Very soon another stone butt appears, its stone floor, like the first one, sunk into the ground. There are, in all, six of these circular hide-outs built for the sportsmen of the past. Lying in a straight line, the butts are all circular with an opening on the lower side; and all are made of slices of millstone grit, the rock which caps Ingleborough, Penyghent and Whernside. It might however, be thought surprising to find it there, between

734709

131

the 1000′ and 1100′ contours, until it is realised that the glaciers at the end of the Ice Age, carried loads of various stones and pebbles and clay, dropping them carelessly as soon as the great thaw came. The way up past the butts is not clearly marked, but these lie beside an easily distinguishable man–made drain, Grey Wife Sike, which used to take water from the upper slopes to the pastures and perhaps to the houses lower down, but which has been allowed to run dry at the lower levels, and now flows freely here only after heavy rains.

735716 After the sixth butt, a ruined shooting box comes into view. Together with the butts it is evidence that once the moor was a heather-covered habitat for grouse, but the heather has been allowed to die (see page 157), and only an occasional brace of grouse will be put up out of the rank yellow grass by unaggressive walkers. After the shooting box the line of butts begins again. Another three of these, and over to the right, across the other side of the 'sike', there is a large boulder,

736717 marked on the map as Harryhorse Stone. However, as Mr Wainwright points out in his almost indispensable *Walks in Limestone Country* (Westmorland Gazette, 1971), the map-maker's eye seems to have erred, and his pen to have strayed, for not a hundred yards further on, and beside the path, there squats a most lifelike model of a little horse, with its large head appealingly leant to one side. A little further on, at about the

737724 1500′ contour, there is a large sinkhole looking like a great grassed-over bomb crater. This is the moment to strike off to the left across the marshy uneven ground, where clumps of bilberry bushes rear up like large hedgehogs in the grass. The area is pitted with sinkholes, sometimes called swallow holes, because surface water, at one time, sank or was swallowed up into the earth at these points. Often, in other parts of the area, these holes are linked by underground tunnels which carry the water away, but this is not the case here, perhaps because the volume of water today is not so very great, and the peaty boggy surface absorbs nearly all of it.

About 100 yards and several sinkholes further on, the first of three remarkable pot holes appears. At this first one, called

734724 Fluted Hole, a perpendicular shaft pierces the limestone, the sides corrugated by falling water and delightfully decorated with ferns and flowers which reach up from ledges towards the light: Hart's Tongue, Spleenwort, various heathers and Herb Robert. A little further on, another flower-bedecked hole, or rather a little collection of holes, Pillar Holes, has five shafts all in a straight line. In one, a thin pillar of limestone inside the shaft rises from a depth of 150 feet. Across the marshy surface and a few yards away, the third of the worthwhile potholes appears, called Long Kin West. This is a linked group of holes spanned by two natural bridges of rock from which one can both see and hear the thin ribbon of a waterfall which tinkles onto the pebbles nearly 300 feet below.

To the south-west, two cairns stand out on the nearby horizon, and to the right of the right-hand cairn, a boundary stone on which a large letter **I** is carved. This indicates no doubt that on that side the parish of Ingleton begins. Here a rough path leads right and left, along the parish boundary. Those who have had enough walking can branch left and walk down to the little hamlet of Cold Cotes, just below the Clapham-Ingleton Road, and so back to Newby. Those who want more should turn right at the cairn. An indistinct track leads up towards Little Ingleborough. Straight ahead, on the left of the track, is what looks like a cliff face. On closer approach it turns out to be the wall of a large roofless shelter for sheep beside the now well-defined path. This leads up the side of Little Ingleborough to the

plateau, which lies a little way beyond the top of this somewhat insignificant little hill. But, insignificant though it may be, it does give a fine view up to Ingleborough, across to Penyghent and down to Gaping Gill. From here too, the paths down from Ingleborough to Horton or Clapham can be clearly seen; equally clear is the way up to the top which leads over the steep boulder-strewn side to the spectacular summit plateau of Ingleborough, once a hill fort said to have been defended by the Brigantes against Roman attacks.

The final assault, even today, makes abnormal demands on the muscles and lungs of a normal walker. With desperate tribesmen defending it, added to the natural difficulties, the Roman soldiers must have found the climb daunting indeed, nor can the objective have been all that tempting. Whichever side held the top, it cannot have been a popular camp-site. Strong winds, mists, hail and snow are common, sweeping across the flat exposed surface of flakey millstone grit and sparse grass. Even with a weatherproof sleeping bag and a waterproof tent, only the hardiest would want to spend a night up there. But some have done it, and the sight of the sun rising from behind Penyghent on a blue and silver morning in high summer is said to be unforgettable.

It has been suggested (see Balderson: *Ingleton Past and Present*, Simpkin Marshall, 1871) that the name Ingleborough indicates that it is the Fire Mountain; and that it gave its name to Ingleton Certainly the flat top, half a mile in circumference, may have been used for centuries as a beacon to pass good or bad news from mountain-top to mountain-top. In 1977 the Queen's jubilee was celebrated here on a damp and misty night with a bonfire. It has been the scene of other celebrations.

In 1830 a party was held on the summit on the occasion of the opening of a tower built there by the Lord of the Manor, Hornby Roughsedge, for use as a shooting lodge and a shelter for shepherds. The day of the opening was fine and sunny; the ceremony attracted crowds from the surrounding farms and villages. There were races, boxing matches and other country contests. Barrels of beer had been rolled up the path, and towards evening the crowd got lively and began literally to 'dilapidate' the tower, dislodging stones and hurling them over the precipice. The ruined tower survived a few years, but today it is no more than a heap of stones. But in the heap it is still possible to see some of the carved stones which formed the base of Roughsedge's tower. The heap is not the only cairn on the top; there is another large one, as well as a trig point and a useful windbreak in the shape of a cross wall, in the middle of which is a useful view-finder which tells you where to look for the Langdale Pikes (visible on a fine still day) or Morecambe Bay. It is said that sometimes one can see the Isle of Man, but I suspect that a telescope might be necessary for this. Probably the most interesting features are the military remains. These have aroused various speculations and interpretations. In their *Ingleton Past and Present* Professor and Margaret Balderson wrote:

> The vestiges of an ancient wall of millstone grit and other rude fortifications are to be seen forming an encircling band close to the verge of this rocky firehill station. It cannot be said that the remains on the top give the slightest evidence of the great engineering skill, resources and technical knowledge of the Romans. Strategically for the purpose the place was good, but the vestiges of the outwork are an insult to Roman energy; the rude fortifications may have been the handiwork of Danes or Britons.

Jacquetta Hawkes in her *Guide to the Prehistoric and Roman Monuments of England and Wales* (1954) is not so impolite about the rude remains. She accepts that the occupiers of the site were probably the Brigantes, but she makes the imaginative and domestic suggestion that the summit of Ingleborough was 'more than a hill fort, it was a hill village where birth and death took place'. Personally I think this overstretches the imagination. The nearest source of water is a few hundred yards down the steep slope from the top, and the icy winds and driving hail and snow would hardly be conducive to village life. Deaths almost certainly have occurred up there, but births? No!

The hill fort theory, then, is backed up by that 'encircling band', the defensive wall, parts of which can still be seen on the eastern side of the circle. It is no ordinary wall, for it consists of great slabs of stone set on end, leaning one against the other. But the second piece of archaeological evidence for the hill fort is seen in the round circles of stones which are not difficult to distinguish in the middle and towards the eastern end of the plateau. These are the very slightly raised outlines of what once were huts, occupied no doubt by the defenders of this surely almost impregnable fortress.

The Greta Valley beloved of
geographers

There are three main exits from the millstone grit cap of
Ingleborough Hill. The first leads back to the popular path and
down to Ingleton via Crina Bottom. The second is the one we
took, coming up from Newby Cote. The path down to Little
Ingleborough forks almost immediately with three prongs.
Straight on, it leads down, via a shooting box, through Sulber
Nick to Horton, where the Three Peak racers on their last long
lap make for the tape. The Newby Cote path slips away to the
right of Little Ingleborough, while over the summit of this little
hill a well-worn track – the middle prong of the fork – leads
down to Gaping Gill, Ingleborough Cave and Clapham (see
page 107).

But it is the third exit from the plateau which points to
Ribblehead. It leads out on the eastern side, starting down a
rock-bestrewn, precipitous path, nasty in icy weather. At the
747748   bottom of the steep slope the path levels out at the corner of the
wall straddled by a wooden stile. Here the path follows the
2000′ contour, and is at first bounded on the right by a friendly
wall. This is made of thin flat slabs of gritstone, shaped rather
like those elliptical Greek pitta loaves. It must have been fairly

136

easy to build, for the slabs seem to stick together and the wall bulges in places without breaking. It often provides welcome shelter from biting winds and hailstones. On the left, the mountain-side slips away down an almost perpendicular slope; the path circles the precipice, swinging round to the left. The official os map of the Three Peaks marks a recommended path directly down the precipice. It would be wiser not to take it! A little more than a mile from the summit, a wall, still in good condition and in no way worried by the very steep slope, comes up from the valley about a thousand feet below, to join our friendly wall. There is a way down beside it; notice how the stones are laid – the courses have to be horizontal, even though the slope leans at 45°. This way leads down to Greak Douk Cave, and from there either to the Hill Inn or eastwards through the Scar Close Nature Reserve, to an excavated Viking or Romano–British settlement, and finally to Ribblehead.

755754

747770

765785

On days when a cloud shrouds the top of Ingleborough, all these places come into view suddenly through the mist; it's an exciting dramatic experience. Perhaps the sun comes out and lights up the south flank of Whernside on the opposite side of the Greta Valley. This valley is beloved of geographers; it is a perfect example of glacial erosion, its flattened U-shape carved by the last of the glaciers 10,000 years ago.

The slowly-moving ice scraped off most of the surface from the upper slopes, exposing the bare bones of limestone, which have flaked and been left as scree. Later, in the valley bottom, enough soil was deposited to provide a shallow bed for pastures through which the river now flows.

Directly below is the little hamlet of Chapel le Dale, sheltered by a few trees. To the left, and where the almost perpendicular precipice begins to level out, there is a great sea of limestone pavement – a wide stretch of clints and grykes. At one time this was a flat surface, scraped smooth by the glacier, but later worked on by rainwater and ice, so that it became cracked and fissured into these strangely regular patterns; for the characteristic of limestone is that it tends to crack at right angles. Up the road from Chapel le Dale is the Hill Inn, not so visible as from the other side of the valley, where we caught sight of it at the end of Kirby Gate (see page 40), but the old Roman Road is clear, straight most of the way from Ingleton to Ribblehead. Some seventeen centuries later it was to become the Lancaster to Richmond turnpike road, and today is merely the B6255.

747770

Some walkers, hungry or thirsty or perhaps just tired, will want to make straight for the inn, but they'll probably pass close to the great crater of Great Douk Cave, for the path down from the wall leads over a stile off to the right towards Great Douk, and the cave is worth at least a brief inspection from the outside. The crater is only about 100 feet deep; ash trees grow up from the bottom, but they can hardly be seen from the approaching path until one is quite close. Inside the perimeter wall at the northern end of the crater there is an easy access path leading down to the wide mouth of the cave, which is overhung with a massive block of limestone. A torrent emerges from this mouth and disappears down a gravelly hole in the middle of the crater. There are two possible ways into the cave, each daunting, involving either a climb up the right-hand side of the waterfall or a crawl along a high ledge and over the top of it. It is classed as a 'beginner's cave'; it is not essential to wear a rubber wet suit to explore it, and after some wallowing and crawling flat on one's stomach one reaches an exit, a hole in the roof, about 500 yards further into the mountain. However, as with almost all the caves in the area, it would be madness for a beginner to attempt it without expert help. Enquiries about this should be made at Whernside Manor, Dent (see page 63).

Hart's Tongue in a gryke

Plants and Flowers

750772

Anyone interested in flowers and plants, or in strange rock formations, should now make for the Scar Close National Nature Reserve. (The address of the Nature Conservancy Council, from whom a permit to enter Scar Close should be obtained, is Archbold House, Archbold Terrace, Newcastle upon Tyne NE2 1EG.) This lies only about 100 yards from the east side of the Great Douk crater. On the near side of a wall is the remains of a water-boiling kiln made of brick, once used no doubt in connection with sheep dipping, as there are some small stone sheep pens branching out from the high wall here. Beside a gate, solid railway sleepers stick out from the wall to make a stile, by which the rough track the other side of the wall can be reached. A few yards away to the left and down the track, on the right-hand side, is a prominent notice board, announcing that Scar Close, just above, is a National Nature Reserve. There is no gated entrance at this point, but it is not too difficult to climb up the natural rock defences. If, however, discretion overcomes valour, the map provided free by the NCC to those who write for a permit will indicate where there is a stile over the wall into the reserve.

A few descriptive paragraphs on the notice board explain the difference between the flora in the grykes and those found on the flat wide tables of limestone, where, most unusually, islands of heather grow thickly in clumps. Once inside, progress should be slow and cautious because of the grykes which may well be concealed under grass or foliage. It's best to take a zig-zag course so as not to miss anything. These flat wide tables of limestone are truly amazing, and might almost serve as billiard table tops; some of them are fifty feet long and almost as wide. Occasionally they are cut into by deep fissures, and they contrast strangely with the lined and pitted clints and grykes a few yards away. After a rainstorm, when the sun comes out from over Lancashire, they shine as if their surface were polished steel or calm water.

Ash and sycamore, as well as bird cherry, have made their way up between the cracks in the limestone pavement, and the deeper cracks have favoured the development of numerous ferns and flowers. Hart's Tongue grows up to an almost luxuriant length, and meadow-sweet gives out a lovely perfume in July and August. Wild raspberries push up, along with honeysuckle,

139

between the clints, but the berries are meagre, and the flowers somewhat stunted. On the more open ground Bloody Cranesbill stands out bright magenta and delicate against the almost white limestone, contrasting strongly with the common rough yellowness of ragwort, often found growing beside it, and both flowering in July and August; Birdseye Primroses (*Primula farinosa*) are found in the patches of grass, looking almost surprised to be there; but it is about the only place to see these. They like the damp limestone just below the surface of the soil. Geoffrey Grigson in his delightful *The Englishman's Flora* (Paladin, 1956) writes, on this occasion somewhat optimistically:

> Visit the Craven Highlands. . . In May and June the small neat flowers of *Primula farinosa* decorate every bank, every slope, every corner between the grey lumps and outcrops of limestone. Finding them for the first time the southerner feels like a plant collector on the Chinese mountains. Through all his life, through all his journeys in China and the mountains of the world, *Primula farinosa* was a favourite with the great collector and the great protagonist of the rock garden, Reginald Farrer [see page 86], who grew up in the shadow of Ingleborough in the West Riding, a country of this primrose.

Grigson is optimistic also about the ubiquitousness of Herb Christopher, known also as Baneberry. He writes:

> Around Ingleborough this plant fills hole after hole between the grey chunks of limestone, or in the grey clefts between the limestone pavements.

This gives the impression that it is almost as common here as Herb Robert. It isn't. I have found it only once, and I'm not saying where. But it is a fascinater. The bright black berries which form after the little white flowers have withered are, as one might expect, baneful. The botanist/apothecary Gerard (1545-1607) warned that the berries were 'deadly and remedyless'.

It may have been more common fifty or a hundred years ago. Walking beyond Scar Close, possibly over Southerscales Scars, Dobson, in his *Rambles by the Ribble*, wrote of:

> the vast plateau of huge blocks of limestone, set with a regularity as if a paviour had placed them there and having

the appearance of a veritable giant's causeway. The aspect was singularly picturesque; here and there through the fissures in the blocks of limestone the ash, the hazel and the alder grew; but while noticing the vegetable inhabitants of the region, I should observe that we also saw, in great abundance, in the fissures of this natural pavement, the Herb Christopher or Baneberry.

I don't want to be a spoil-sport, but I've not found Herb Christopher growing on Southerscales Scar. Botanists are perhaps a little like keen fishermen – not only optimistic and tending to exaggeration, but also ecstatic when they make a catch. Dobson describes well the enthusiasm of his botanist companion on the lower plateau of Ingleborough:

> We had reached the summit of the lower hill and the character of the soil was quite changed; instead of limestone

we were on a patch of moss. . . . There were ling, some
crowberry, the whortleberry and lots of what my friend had
long been in search of, the mountain bramble, or cloudberry,
in bloom, and notwithstanding the bleakness of its
inhabitation and the lateness of the season, its delicate white
petals were fully expanded. It was almost as plentiful on this
plateau as buttercups in a meadow in summer. . .

I shall never forget the ecstacies of delight in which my
friend indulged on his discovery. Had my friend been a little
younger he would have been imitating Tom Scott in the Old
Curiosity Shop, and standing on his head. . . That quaint old
botanist Gerard says of the cloudberry 'These plants are
called in the north of England where they especially doe
grow, knot berries or knout berries. Knot berries do love
open snowie hills and mountains. . .'

Evidently Gerard was told by a Lancashire 'simpler', Thomas
Hesketh, that it was called Cloudberry, because it grew on the
tops of Pendle in Lancashire and Ingleborough 'where the
clouds are lower than the tops of the same all winter long,
whereupon the people of the country call them Cloud Berries'.
As Grigson points out, the truth is that it means Hill Berry,
from the Old English *clud* meaning hill.

The Early Purple Orchid is not uncommon on the lower
slopes of Ingleborough towards Ribblehead, and it is a welcome
announcer that spring has come; indeed in some years it is in
flower at the same time as the wood anemone and Lesser
Celandine and the huge snowdrops which can be found in the
woods but which persist here very much later than in the south.
I've sometimes wondered whether *The Times* would take a
letter from me headed 'The Last Snowdrop', affirming that my
snowdrops were blooming in June.

The Early Purple Orchid (*Orchis mascula*) is associated with a
whole string of not-so-old wives' tales, all emanating from the
form and condition of two root tubers, one of which is firm and
full, the other flaccid and empty, the tubers supplying the name
orchid, from the Greek *orchis*, testicle. Grigson gives some
fascinating information about the uses to which it was put,
quoting from an English translation of a German manual, *The
vertuouse boke of Distyllacyon* (1527). Here one can read the
instructions for use of the water obtained from distilling the full
tubers: 'In the mornynge and at nyght dronke of the same water

at eche tyme an ounce and a halfe causeth great hete, therefore it geveth lust unto the workes of generacyon and multiplicacyon of sperma.' But in the next paragraph, Grigson is kind enough to assure readers that 'in fact the tubers of *Orchis mascula* are altogether without the power attributed to them'.

Hereabouts too, close beside or even in the streams that come off the sides of the hill, and on the lower slopes, as early as March but lasting into May, the Marsh Marigolds (or Molly Bobs or King Cups) abound, especially if it has been a very wet February. Much later their less blatant and more sophisticated friend, but no close relation, the Globe Flower appears in the wet grass. In late summer my favourite can be found, Grass of Parnassus, standing erect among reedy grasses, proudly displaying its one perfect flower, a white five-petalled cup with slight green veins.

Time now to move back to Scar Close and make for the exit over a stile at the eastern end. After the stile a path leads eastwards to a strange wood of closely planted larch, with a few sycamore interspersed. This is known as Garlic Wood. Although I've not found wild garlic there, it certainly grows easily in the area. It's called Stink Rods locally, so it's unlikely that locals would use it for flavouring their salads. In fact, though, if you chop the leaves and stalks fine like parsley, it's a good substitute for the real thing.

760784

At the eastern end of Garlic Wood, sheltered from view and from the wild west winds by a bank of glacial rubble and shale, is one of the most interesting archaeological sites in the area. It was excavated in 1975-6, the work being urgently undertaken because Amey Roadstone, the owners of the Ribblehead Limestone Quarry, had recently been given planning permission to extend quarrying to take in and break up the site.

765785

Here are outlines of three buildings, each opening onto a common 'yard'. It was supposedly a farm settlement, one of several in the area, and occupied by several families. Dating is difficult. Some say that it is Viking in origin, the invaders coming over from Ireland, having landed on the Lancashire coast; others suggest that it was built and lived in by Anglians who came from across the North Sea at a much earlier date.

The main building is about 20 yards long and 4 yards across. There is an opening at each end. Due north of the main building is a smaller one where, in a corner, traces of a kiln or oven and the presence of animal bones as well as the matching top and bottom stones of a quern (see page 53), led the diggers to the conclusion that this was the cooking place. The third building lies slightly further away to the north-west of the main building, and this has been dubbed the workshop, on the discovery of iron-rich cinders near the central hearth. Two iron knife blades were found outside the northern doorway of the main building. Among other finds were four coins, all from the third quarter of the ninth century. (A detailed report of the dig and a discussion of the significance of the discoveries can be read in the Council of British Archaeology Research Report No. 27 by A. King.)

The site is only a few hundred yards from Ribblehead. By skirting the eastern end of the quarry (which lies to the north of the site) and joining the road which links the quarry to the main road, it is not difficult to find a way to the Station Inn. After this walk even the most energetic would be advised to time their arrival during normal opening hours.

764791

15 October

All night the rain had lashed the windows and in the morning it was still chucking it down. The becks were roaring full, new streams in new channels carried away the extra tons of water that had fallen on the tops. The usual channels, underground, had got blocked with water, and somehow it had to find an unaccustomed overground route to the Ribble. Everywhere around, famous waterfalls deserved a special visit and new ones called noisily for attention while they lasted.

In the afternoon the rain was still falling, but I thought I would go and see what was happening along a little valley which is a favourite of mine in summer. At the top there's a grove of Botticellian delight where, on a fine sunny day, all that is missing from the patch of greensward are the dancing muses diaphanously draped. In summer the grass is decorated with Eye Bright or Bright Eyes (Germander Speedwell is its uglier but better-known name) and buttercups. The grove is half-circled by a stream which makes it into a peninsula. Two or three huge Scotch pines, a plane tree and some mountain ash have safely grown there. Like the flowers and grasses they are protected by the stream, and at the opposite end by an enclosing bank and rock face, from grazing sheep and cows.

From the base of the rock on a normal day the stream swirls out of a wide, rather inviting cave mouth. Curving round the peninsula, it darts away at one corner towards the valley between high cliff walls. Adding to the fun of the place, a second stream joins the one from the cave mouth before it corners; this one sweeps over a long lip of flat limestone, falling in a pretty waterfall gracefully into the main stream.

I've often thought what an ideal place this would be for a couple to camp on a summer night; or a small family – a marvellous time the children would have, lighting a fire and

cooking, then washing in the stream and going to sleep in their tent while mum and dad talked in soft voices outside. But camping wouldn't be allowed. Pity.

Today, even in wellingtons, it was impossible to get at all close to the mouth of the cave. Water gushed from it under pressure, the grass was bare of flowers and the broad flat lip of that graceful waterfall was a moving mass of foaming brown water which roared into the stream below. Above it and to the side there was a grassy patch with no trees; here half a dozen cows were lying peacefully chewing in the rain. I moved downstream along the rocky tree-lined bank; the water tossed itself over rocks; a long-dead tree had been carried down with the floodwater and had got stuck between two rocks, its black fingers at the end of the dead branches twitched and stretched out as the water sucked and pulled at the trapped trunk.

Lower down, the stream passes through some calm green meadows. Here the water ran deep and fast, but smooth now, and dark – almost silent. At a bend a great shale bank rose out of the water like a dead whale, stuck there. But there was a roaring ahead at the end of the meadow. This was the whirlpool. A clump of trees sheltered a wide basin. New streams poured into it from three sides. In summer this is a dump – blue plastic fertiliser bags, old bicycles, tin baths, old motor tyres, all litter the stones through which a few grasses and stunted trees poke their way up. One stream only feeds it, but disappears under the stones as if disgusted.

Today the surface was a seething mass of water. In the middle a fully grown ash tree, heavy with seed pods, was awash, the brown water reaching half way up its trunk. Round the rim of the whirlpool the froth from the waterfalls had collected, forming huge brown and yellow bolsters of bubbles. In one spot, near where the water had found an exit, it passed under a long lump of foam, whose whole surface was heaving and throbbing like a huge yeasty slug in labour.

I trudged off home, weary but rewarded. It was my birthday.

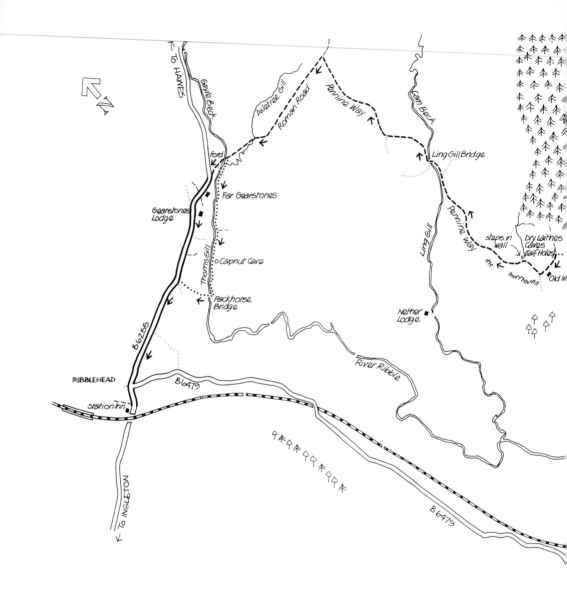

Horton viewed from Bracken
Bottom

Chapter 5 Up Penyghent and down to Ribblehead

For many people Penyghent is the favourite of the Three. It doesn't show itself off like Ingleborough; while Whernside, although the highest, and possessing a name of interest to philologists, is pretty dull to look at – a great sleeping worm, although on certain rare days, with a sprinkling of snow on the top and a pale blue sky behind, it becomes beautiful. But Penyghent. . .

It is the lowest of the Three, at 2,277 feet. But might this not prove an attraction? It lies comfortably feline beside the infant Ribble. Its name must arouse curiosity. The other two Peaks have names which are easily explained. Ingleborough has been translated as the Fire Mountain, indicating, according to Professor Balderson, in his *Ingleton Past and Present* (Simpkin Marshall, 1871), its use as a beacon as far back as the Roman occupation. A source of whetstones and querns is the prosaic explanation for Whernside (see page 53). But Penyghent, Hill of the Winds, has a romantic ring; Merlin himself might have christened it.

And wind-swept it can be. That long western flank, and in particular the high rock fortress at the southern end, receives the full force of the prevailing Atlantic gales. They blow in from Morecambe Bay and bite into the rocks and screes, sweeping the snows of winter and spring onto and over the straight spine, where they lie in drifts often into the months which we optimistically call summer. Not only walkers, but cavers, rock-climbers and occasionally skiers happily use Penyghent for their sport. Once it produced limestone and coal for the kilns along its sides, and still it provides delight for flower-lovers – perhaps especially for the non-experts – with that curtain of purple saxifrage which drapes the western cliff in late April. 'Like aubretia on a garden wall' suggests Wainwright (in *Walks in Limestone Country*). And the green pastures of the lower slopes continue to offer nourishment (whether as grass or hay) for herds of sheep and cattle. So it is a friendly mountain. Some say it looks like a sleeping tiger, some like a sphinx; but whatever it may resemble it is very climbable.

One good place to start is the little hamlet of Brackenbottom, half a mile to the south of Horton, just off the Settle road. But on the way is a little detour, much recommended. From Horton a start can be made at the less-used lych gate of Horton Church, taking either of the two small parallel roads which go along each bank of Horton Beck just before it reaches the village. The aim of this little detour is to visit one of the most enchanting natural scenes in the whole area, Douk Gill Cove. It is a Malham Cove in miniature; it is not ostentatious nor awe-inspiring; its proportions and setting are both magnificent and humane. However, it lies in private land at the far end of a meadow, so it is important to get permission to view. The owner's farmhouse is beside Horton Beck at the side of the left-hand road going up from the church, just opposite the footbridge.

The meadow in question is reached by taking the right-hand road, now enclosed by trees. Entry can be made through a gate just after the road bends round to the right towards Brackenbottom. Walking round the left-hand edge of the field and along the bank of the beck, one comes to a low, well-made wall which offers prominent jutting-out stones to form a stile which is easy to climb without causing damage. Immediately in front the cove appears: formed by a dark cyclorama of high rock, topped and surrounded by trees, and decorated with all kinds of plants and shrubs growing up both from the wet ground and out of the face of that great limestone wall. Water pours down, or just trickles from it, depending on the amount of rain at Horton on the previous day or two.

A certain Frederick Riley, author of *The Ribble from its Source to the Sea* (John Heywood, 1914), wrote of the 'romantic Douk Gill Scar', which he visited just before the first war:

> This beetling crag of limestone, upreared amidst the surrounding trees and tangled undergrowth, forms a most striking picture. What the scene must have been when the water poured over the scar – as it undoubtedly has done – is left for the imagination to conceive. The stream now issues from a cave-like opening in the face of the rock, where the

812721

813723

816724

816726

water makes its appearance after a long underground journey. Numerous ferns and flowering plants are here met with, the moss covered and flower bedecked boulders forming a wild natural rock garden.

It is stupid to try and go over the fields from the cove to Brackenbottom, because it means going over a number of high and unpredictable walls. Anyhow there is no Right of Way. So it is best to return to the road and go up it towards Brackenbottom. Just before the first building a signpost points through a gate to a path on the right of a wall, while another notice firmly warns walkers not to take a nearby path to the left, once wrongly recommended by some guidebooks. The correct path is well trodden, this being a favourite route for the Three Peakers. The start is over grass punctuated with limestone outcrops; a convenient stile leads over a wall in front, and the path continues gently upwards; but soon, underfoot, a stretch of

Douk Gill

some will be dead, others will need attention. Orphan lambs will be carried (by their front legs, not 'on a shoulder gently laid') back to the farm kitchen to be given a bottle of warm milk to suck, traditionally laced with whisky; they are kept warm until they are strong and the weather improves. Sheepdogs are of course as vital today to the farm economy as they ever were. They are usually Border Collies. To an 'incomer' they all seem miraculously trained and obedient to their master's voice or his special whistle. The time to differentiate them is at the local sheep dog trials which take place, often in front of a tiny local group of spectators, from April through to October.

Except for the orphans, all the new lambs are kept together with their mothers for about a month in the 'in-bye' land, close to the farms. Those with one lamb are then put up on the moor, while those with twins are kept in the pastures. On some farms about a third have twins, though there are farmers who prefer not to encourage twins.

Almost all the male lambs in their first few weeks of life are castrated, the exceptions being those which look strong and especially healthy, and therefore may be expected to become good breeders. By September, most of the castrated lambs are either sold to farmers in the lowlands of Yorkshire or Lancashire or sold 'fat' to butchers. But most of the females – 'gimmer hoggs' as they are called until their first sheering at one year old – are kept for future flock replacements.

The upper slopes of the moor, above the enclosed pastures, are rough grazing areas, and are usually shared out among a group of farmers (the 'graziers') who own the grazing rights in common. Their rights are 'stinted', that is to say each has the right to a fixed number of 'gaits', which he has paid for. One gait represents the right to graze one sheep; four gaits are needed for a cow. A gait in 1980 cost from £3 to £4 a year, depending on the state of the land. At one time the farmers concerned paid a shepherd to watch the stock for them all; he saw to it that the gaits were respected. But the shepherds have died out and have not been replaced; one result is that there are strong suspicions that certain farmers put more stock on the grazing areas than their gaits should permit. The sheep of each farmer are branded with the owner's initials on their horns, and also by a coloured marking fluid on the wool.

By late spring or early summer, all stock are taken out of the meadows to let the grass grow to a decent length. The hay used to be stored in isolated barns in the pastures. These are a feature of the Dales. The local name for them is 'laithes', and here not only is the hay stored, but cows are accommodated too, so the laithes are also 'shippons' (cowsheds). In the past the cows would be brought there each evening for milking, the hay being stored in the loft above so it could easily be thrown down to them. Also the muck from the shippon could easily be taken from the ground floor and spread on the surrounding pasture. The only really hard work came after milking, when the milk would be carried in 'back cans' across the fields to the farmhouse dairy. A can held from five to eight gallons of milk and looked like the container used by *vignerons* on the continent when they spray their vines. Before the First War, most of the milk was made into butter or cheese on the farm and sold in the markets; it is said you could tell the cheese of one farm from another by the 'provven' that had been fed to the cows, but it was all Wensleydale cheese. The Buttertubs, very deep cylindrical holes beside the road between Hawes and Muker, were so called because the farmers from Muker, on their way back from Hawes market, used to keep their unsold butter there, hung in baskets in the cold air of the Buttertubs, until they passed there on their way back to Hawes the following week. Between the Wars, the production of farm cheese gradually declined; the Milk Marketing Board was set up, and milk was sold at a steadier price, while the Wensleydale cheese was more and more made in the factories at Hawes and Settle.

Today, as explained above, EEC policies have led to a decline in milk production, and this has meant that the breed of cattle has altered. Most of the cows to be seen today are still black with a few white markings, as a result of the import in the past of Friesian dairy bulls. Over several decades these were mated with the traditional dairy Shorthorns which were roan-coloured. However, as beef production replaced milk, Herefords replaced the Friesian bulls, and this is resulting in more red-coloured calves. Now the fashion has changed again and it is not uncommon to see the creamy-coloured Charollais bulls (and more recently still, Limousins) stomping round the fields. No doubt therefore the colour of the calves will change yet again in a few years.

The bull is usually left with the cows for specified periods, so that the calves can be born at convenient intervals; often this is in late spring or in August. Cows go on heat every three weeks and their gestation period is nine and a half months.

There have been changes too in the breeds of sheep, or, more strictly speaking, in the breeds of tups (rams). Traditionally the flocks were either Dalesbred or Swaledale – the former to be recognised by their totally black faces, relieved by a white patch above each nostril, while the Swaledales have a white muzzle, going grey as they get older, the rest of the face being black. But today other breeds have been introduced, especially Hexham and Leicestershire tups with their long legs and prominent, almost Roman noses. More recently, and again no doubt influenced by the Common Market, Texel rams have been brought in from Holland, for they are reputed to father lambs with a high proportion of tender lean meat – in fact the local butcher may well assure you that the leg of local lamb you're buying was sired by a Texel, and will therefore be lean and tender.

The ewes are 'tupped' in November, usually one tup to about fifty sheep, though some can cope with as many as eighty. He stays with one lot of ewes for about three weeks and is then passed on to another lot. Sometimes the ram gets tired, and has to be replaced by a 'reserve' after a couple of weeks. The ram is normally 'ruddled', that is, marked with a transferable powder on his under-belly, so that the farmer can tell which sheep have been tupped. How many readers of *The Return of the Native* realise for what purpose the reddleman, in the second chapter, was peddling his 'redding'? In those days only one colour was used – a reddy brown. Today, after the tup has been with the sheep for a week, the colour is changed, so that the lambing time of each ewe can be predicted. And modern methods of ruddling have been introduced; a little harness is strapped onto the ram to which a marking crayon is attached, the colour of which is easily rubbed off onto the ewe's backside when they get together.

In the summer the ewes are clipped and dosed against 'worm' and liver fluke, not uncommon on these marshy pastures and moors, and in October the whole flock is dipped to kill off the external parasites, and protect them against sheep scab.

The hay harvest is important. Every three to five years the

meadows are spread with lime and basic slag, and usually every year with F.Y.M. (farm yard manure) from the shippons. The first grass from the meadows is eaten by the young lambs and their mothers so that normally only one crop of hay is produced, and this has to be cut whenever a fine spell offers a chance to get it in dry. This may be in June, but if the summer is wet, cutting might be delayed till September. The unpredictable weather, when a day of ceaseless rain may well be followed by a bright and cloudless tomorrow, has meant that some farmers, because of the risks involved in leaving the hay to dry in the fields, are making the grass into silage. Some too have artificial drying barns. But whatever they do, because of the increase in stock (some would call it 'overstocking'), they very seldom have enough hay of their own to last the whole winter. So lorry loads of baled hay can often be seen on the roads in the autumn delivering to the farms from the more clement east and south, adding perhaps ten or fifteen percent to the necessary winter feed.

The average size of a farm hereabouts varies greatly, depending on the quality of the land; the farmer and his family are seldom helped by more than one worker. The work is demanding, but very varied, and as long as subsidies for hill farms offer them a reasonable living, most of them find it worth sticking at.

Now that we know that those sandwich grabbing sheep on Penyghent belong to a farmer who has bought gaits up there, it's time to leave the grassy (or snowy) summit of the Hill of the Winds. The way towards Ribblehead is clear. For about half a mile the path leads down northwards, steep at first, as the millstone grit gives way to limestone. It hugs the side of the mountain, which falls away abruptly on the left. This steep slope is partly grassed over and partly spread with light grey scree. This is where the purple saxifrage pours out of the ground for a week or two in April.

838742   Ahead and half left two possible routes are clear to see. The one is a badly worn track over the peat; it turns sharp left from the path we are on. The other, which today is the recommended route for the Three Peaks racers, leads off less sharply to the left. Both go down to meet Hull Pot Beck. The more worn track is a reminder of the real dangers of tourism, and of a particular walk becoming too popular. By 1980 that path over the peat had become a quagmire after being trodden down in all weathers by thousands of walking boots. The Yorkshire Dales National Park has now come to the rescue, organising groups of young volunteers who have worked hard and successfully to repair the damage by building sikes (drainage channels), establishing a parallel alternative path where necessary and providing little bridges of thick planks over the 'sikes'.

Those who follow this repaired track are in for a pleasant surprise, a surprise which may well be heard before it is seen. For behind a wire enclosure (to keep out sheep), and invisible

826740   from the path (but, after rains, not inaudible), is Hunt Pot – an evil-looking slit in the rock surface, only six feet across and three times as long. Water from the stream pours over a lip of rock and splashes to the bottom, 200 feet below. It is not too dangerous, if great care is taken, to make a little exploration around the lip of the hole, but from whatever point of vantage one peers downwards, there is no chance of seeing the bottom.

The track continues gently downwards, passing a line of disused shooting butts. For this was once a grouse moor, until the heather was burned too close to the ground, and the sheep could get at the new shoots in the spring and damage the roots. (The heather hasn't grown again.) A small stone hut, once used

823744   as a shooting box but now roofless, marks the end of the track. To the left, through a gate, a bridle way leads pleasantly back to Horton, following the Pennine Way to the Crown Inn. But this

166

would be a diversion. For those who are aiming at Ribblehead, and those of a healthy curiosity, Hull Pot must not be missed.

824746   This unusual pothole lies a few hundred yards to the right, up a grassy path leading to another wire enclosure which may stop sheep falling into the very large limestone basin 100 yards long, 60 feet across and 60 feet deep. Hull Pot Beck pours into it after heavy rain, and it is said that after continuous rain over a number of days the whole basin fills up. It must be an impressive sight, and worth walking up from Horton to see. The waters from here come out at Douk Gill (see page 152), while those from Hunt Pot, crossing the Hull Pot waters somewhere en route without merging, come out at Brants Gill above Horton. (Such odd subterranean routes have been discovered by pouring dye into the streams at the upper end, and watching the relevant colours emerge at the other.)

Those who decide to resist the temptation of returning to Horton should continue past Hull Pot and up the left-hand side of the beck for a few hundred yards until they can see a ladder

826750   stile over the wall on the right. This is where the Three Peaks racers come down from Penyghent, interested only in the shortest route to Ribblehead, and not in Hunt or Hull Pots. They leap across the stream and race on over the moor towards Black Dub Moss. The next part of the trip is tricky, for Black Dub Moss, which the unwary might be tempted to negotiate, is treacherous. In fact the organisers of the race in wet years arrange for flags to be placed along the route here to guide runners away from this evil-sounding quagmire. (Was it once thought of as Black Tub?) One year, on the day before the race, a steward prospecting the route sank up to his elbows in Black Dub before being hauled out by friends.

But the walk across this wild bit of wuthering country is an experience; and it is easiest to follow the way taken by the racers. After leaving the beck the track goes over the moor to a

821754   wall with a stile leading to the dreaded quagmire. Cross the stile and keep left, skirting the bog; after topping a rise, another wall

815754   comes into view, with a gate; go through the gate and down the

810754   slope to where the path joins the Pennine Way. It also joins the route I've suggested for those doing the side of Penyghent, but for only about half a mile (see page 192). Here, turning north, it is best to keep to the Pennine Way, which after crossing two

813772   small streams is signposted a little further on. The finger points

804774   down the hill to Old Ing. This is a long farmhouse with laithe and shippon built on, but the living quarters have been abandoned. About a hundred years ago the family moved to the separate, more respectable-looking but less picturesque house which stands across the yard from the long barn.

On the roadside near Old Ing another Pennine Way signpost points along a track leading north, a pleasing track because it sticks to the 1150′ contour, and offers fine views of Ingleborough and Whernside. About 100 yards along the track from Old Ing, steps in the wall on the right lead immediately to a remarkable slit in the ground. It is called Dry Laithes Cave, but also goes under another name, Calf Holes. It can't be a place where calves drank; more likely they occasionally fell down the thirty feet to the gravelly bottom, just as the stream, coming in from the top, continuously does. Evidently the water travels on through a cave system underground to reach Browngill Cave, half a mile away to the south.

804776

Thorns Gill

The track leads to the top end of Ling Gill. Just before this point a notice board beside the wall on the left declares Ling Gill to be a Nature Reserve, protected by the Nature Conservancy Council (see page 139). There is a stile over the wall at this point but anyone expecting to explore this wild and fascinating gorge won't be able to get more than a glimpse of it from the safe side of the fence which the Conservancy Council have erected to save the lives of sheep, and possibly of enthusiastic humans.

However, no permit is required to enter Ling Gill, and the very active and intrepid might consider attacking it from the top, especially in summer when there is only a little water in the stream.

The track now curves round the upper end of Ling Gill to cross the stream, Cam Beck, over a remarkable old stone bridge with a stone set in the parapet whose carved figures and letters can just be deciphered. **ANNO 1765** is the heading: then **THIS BRIDGE WAS REPAIRED AT THE CHARGE OF THE WHOLE WEST RIDING**. The bridge and the inscription are evidence that the road was once an important one, and the width of the bridge an indication that not only horses and foot-sloggers were expected to cross it, but carts travelling from Settle in the south to join the Roman road, less than a mile from the bridge, leading west to Bainbridge (a fortified Roman strongpoint until the 4th century AD), and east to Ingleton, Ribchester and the coast. (Ribchester, now a small village, was once a Roman stronghold between Preston and Carlisle.) This last is the route I now recommend. After the bridge the track follows Cam Beck for a short distance. The water here flows fast and smoothly over wide flat limestone rocks; it will get a surprise after passing under the bridge, when it tumbles and splashes and swirls over waterfalls and in whirlpools as it makes its noisy way down Ling Gill.

The track soon leaves the stream, striking out left across the moor. After less than a mile it joins the Roman road at a T-junction. The way to Ribblehead leads left down the hill for half a mile and then bends to the right, crossing Axletree Gill before reaching the valley of the embryo Ribble at Gayle Beck. But why Axletree Gill? One explanation is because the beck frequently wore great ruts across the road after rains, and so caused many a cart's axle to snap; the tractors which occasionally roar up the Roman road today are tougher. At
Gayle Beck there is a useless footbridge to the left of the track,

built originally by the Lord of the Manor for his shooting parties. Once it had three sections, but the third has been washed away and it is doubtful if it will ever be replaced. But the ford at the bottom of the track is almost always passable on foot, and the track up the other side leads directly onto the main Hawes–Ribblehead road.

The road bends to the left, and a drive leads down to Far Gearstones farm, nestling under high trees. A little further along on the left is an interesting building, a barn, in which the stones of the walls are laid at a slight angle so that they all lean outwards, allowing any water which might seep through into the inner filling of rubble to drip towards the outside. But, strangely, the stones are cut so that the outer edge, the face of the wall, is perfectly flat. The phenomenon is called water-chocked. In this building it can easily be seen since the window spaces contain no windows, and the tilted stones are clearly visible where they form the upright side of the window spaces.

The road continues past Gearstones Lodge on the left, now an outdoor pursuits centre for a big school at Mirfield, near Huddersfield. On the opposite side, a building has recently been pulled down. This was the ancient Gearstones Inn, which lost its licence in 1911. Rumour still relates that the magistrate who decided the case was the Lord of the Manor, and he thought that his tenants were behind with their rents largely because they spent too much time playing dominoes at Gearstones and not enough on their farms. The pub got a low rating from that tireless traveller, the Honourable John Byng, Viscount Torrington (see page 19), who stopped there in June 1792 and wrote in his diary, after a journey on horseback from Askrigg in the company of a Mr Blakey:

> Crossing a ford Mr Blakey led me to a public house called Gierstones [sic], the seat of misery in a desert; the Scotch fair held upon the heath added to the horror of the curious scenery, the ground in front of the house crowded by Scotch cattle and drovers, and the house crowded by the buyers and sellers, most of whom were in plaids, filibegs [short kilts], etc. My friend who knew the house forced his way through the lower floor and interned himself in the only wainscotted room upstairs where at last we procured some boiled slices of stale pork and some fry'd eggs with some wretched beer and brandy. The only custom of this hotel, or rather hovel, is

derived from grouse shooters and from two Scotch fairs. At the conclusion of the long squabble, the two nations agree in mutual drunkenness. The Scotch are always wrapped in their plaids, a defence against heat, cold or wet, but they, the plaids, are a prevention of speed or activity, so whenever any cattle strayed they instantly threw down their plaid that they might overtake them.

The pub also did good trade during the building of the viaduct and Blea Moor Tunnel (see page 68). In fact it was here that the young Midland Railway engineer Charles Sharland, when surveying the route for the Settle–Carlisle line, was cut off with six colleagues by snowdrifts for three weeks in 1869. They finally tunnelled their way out through the snow.

The Station Inn at Ribblehead also dates from about that time, and serves hungry and thirsty travellers and locals rather better than Gearstones in the 18th century.

Cave at Ribblehead

For those who don't feel like tramping down to Ribblehead by the road, there is a way down beside Gayle Beck. It includes one of the more surprising little beckside walks, along Thorns Gill – for the waters of Gayle Beck, before becoming the Ribble at Ribblehead, have a brief life under that name, taken no doubt from the abandoned farm of Thorns between Gearstones and Nether Lodge. This route avoids the crossing of Gayle Beck by the ford mentioned on page 170, although the way along the side of the left bank is rough until the little iron footbridge is reached. Here Thorns Gill begins, fully justifying Wainwright's praise of this little glen:

782797

> A paradise of exquisite beauty . . . a series of waterfalls and deep pools between eroded limestone cliffs and steep banks gloriously adorned with hanging gardens of wild flowers. . . Please be content to appreciate them in their natural habitat and leave them undisturbed. Amongst the wealth of varieties are seen the rare globe flower, bird's eye primrose and fragrant orchid growing in happy profusion. (*Walks in Limestone County*)

Half way down the left bank of the stream is Capnut Cave, which can be explored for a few hundred yards without too much inconvenience by those with a torch and who don't mind getting their feet wet. Above the cave and in the meadows beside the stream further on there are some fine examples of huge limestone boulders perched on pedestals, abandoned by the last of the melting glaciers 10,000 years ago. The end of Thorns Gill is marked by a picturesque little stone footbridge, wide enough only for a packhorse and its master to cross. From here a path across the bridge and through the fields joins the main road only a few hundred yards from Ribblehead and the Station Inn. End of walk.

776795

22 November

It had rained all morning, and the field beside the house had streamed down until the water collected into one deep channel and dived underground before reaching the house. I got soaked just going up the hill 300 yards to unblock the damned water source.

In the late afternoon it was still windy but sunny through gaps in the clouds, and when I went out, making for the Witchwood by the lower field, the sky was a palette of colours. Across the great western gap, over where Morecambe Bay must be, there was stretched a narrow strip of bright orange sky – cream and orange actually – and it pierced the jagged stones of the wall between it and me, filtered as if through an irregular sieve. Above the bright strip, lying flat on the strip, there were soft complete clouds, forming a red and brown blanket, a long duvet rather, and then higher up the red and brown merged with ill-defined patches of grey where the sunlight couldn't reach properly. But further on still, above my head and stretching east towards Penyghent, the cloud cover became elongated strips of battleship blue, until as they reached the great high flank of the mountain they darkened to black.

I walked across tussocks and rocks through a conglomeration of sheep who looked at me curiously out of their black faces, simple and trusting, so not bothering to run away. Their heavy trailing fleeces matched the scabby rocks. These served as stepping stones and it felt like walking on acne. As I got near the wood the wind totally dropped, so there was no sound from the trees. And looking over the wall onto the dark under-tree floor I noticed a large dog streaking away: no, not a dog of course, a large leggy fox. I clambered over the round-stone wall (why *round* here? It must have been ground into that shape by once

having been in a river bed) and stepped onto the mossy, grassy floor under the green-trunked, green-branched larch trees, all overgrown with grey-green lichen. The slits between the rocks on the floor, the grykes, were full of lush Hart's Tongues, whole bunches of them still green. Under the trees, stooping low and jumping across the gaps, I arrived on that giant's table of split rocks stretching from west to east. One fissure, eight feet deep, stretches unbroken for at least thirty yards. At the eastern end, the further end of it, a huge tongue-shaped boulder is loosely wedged between the sides level with the tabletop, and as I balanced on it, first leaning west then east, a deep boom boom emerged from below me as its sides knocked against its containing rock walls.

I climbed down over the boulders at the end onto a short narrow path between great clumps of limestone, standing together like grey gigantic cottage loaves, some of them with separate flat tops of limestone placed neatly and firmly on their tops – solid grey tam o'shanters! Then up again along another narrow path between more boulders. From the top of the last one I looked back down on the boulders strewn around haphazard; one like Ozymandias, flat on his back, two fat, chopped-off legs emerging from his long fat belly – but no head! So back along the topside of the wood across the reddish-brown reedy grass, and through the inquisitive sheep. This farmer daubs each one with a large patch of greyish blue to distinguish them from his neighbour's (who daubs his russet brown). This is important as the sheep do get mixed up sometimes when a bit of wall tumbles because some 'hated hikers' haven't bothered to use the stile, or have failed to shut a gate.

These sheep match the rocks, and the grass matches the sky and another bit of the sky matches the rocks. Then suddenly, just before the light goes, round the corner of the wood I see the viaduct lit up, bright in the final beam from the disappearing sun, and a white farmhouse the other side of the valley turns red. The orange strip of sky beyond Morecambe Bay has by now moved off southwards, and a point of clear orange is actually the sinking sun. This is what has lit up the viaduct. In two more minutes it is below the western rim, and has left jagged darkened clouds perched there, each black cloud not silver-lined but truly gold-lined. What a walk!

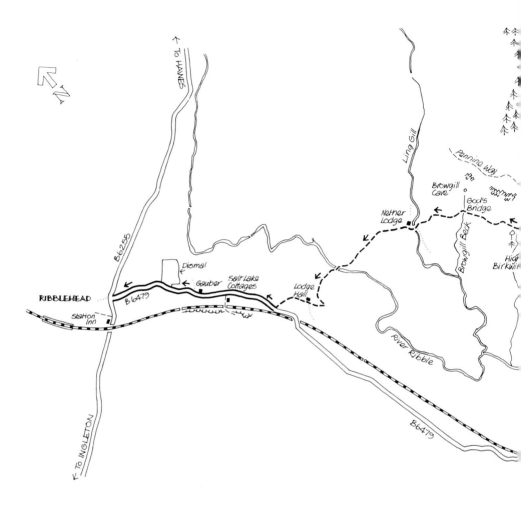

N

TO HAWES

B6255

Ling Gill

Pennine Way

Browgill
Cave

God's
Bridge

Nether
Lodge

Browgill Beck

High
Birkwi

Dismal

Gauber

Salt Lake
Cottages

Lodge
Hall

RIBBLEHEAD

B6479

Station
Inn

River Ribble

TO INGLETON

B6479

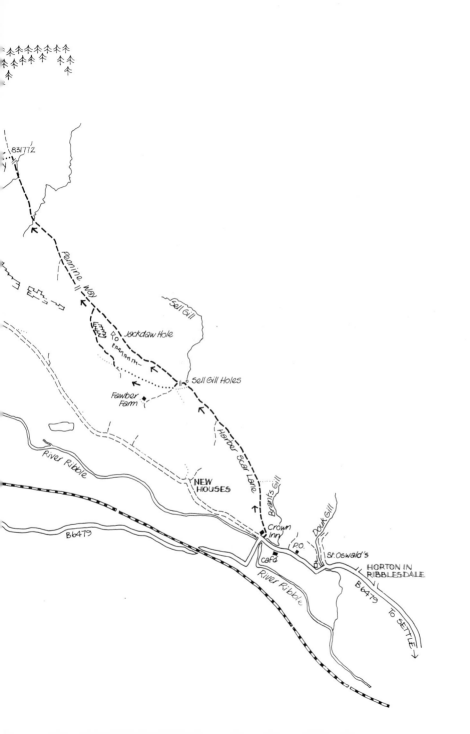

831772

Pennine Way

Sell Gill

Jackdaw Hole

Sell Gill Holes

Fawber Farm

River Ribble

Harber Scar Lane

NEW HOUSES

River Ribble

B6479

Brants Gill

Douk Gill

Crown Inn

P.O.

Café

St. Oswald's

HORTON IN RIBBLESDALE

B6479

TO SETTLE →

The Blue Lagoon at Horton

Chapter 6   To Ribblehead by the Side of Penyghent

807727   A start can conveniently be made at the Crown at Horton, now the only pub in the village. This was not always so. At the other end of the village, opposite the church, was once the Golden Lion. It was bought a few years ago by Foxwood School in Leeds as an annexe and outdoor pursuits centre (a take-over more appreciated by the school than by the village!). There are three bridges; two older ones, one of which takes the road across Brants Gill, and the other, near the church, which carries it over Douk Gill. The third bridge crosses the Ribble, and is not so old; this suggests that perhaps the old road did not cross the river here, but went straight on, up the narrow road to New Houses, High Birkwith and eventually to Gearstones and the Roman road. This theory is confirmed by one of the earliest maps of Yorkshire drawn by T. Jefferys, dated 1772, which marks the High Birkwith road, but no way up the right bank to Selside and Ribblehead.

Horton today does not deserve the reputation suggested by its Norse name, *Hor-tun*, the Village-in-the-Mud. It is in fact rather a spick-and-span little place, with a large car park and a camping field, which point to the importance of the tourist invasion at weekends and especially during the spring and summer.

There is a mixture of buildings. Some are very ordinary, built about 50 years ago; some rather pretentious, trying to look old but only recently put up (these have been described as lamb dressed as mutton); and some are fine examples of traditional Dales buildings, long and low with small windows and prominent porches roofed by two huge single slates. Porches are a feature of houses in the Dales, and must have seemed the more necessary when, as was once common, the front door opened directly into the front room, known as the houseroom or

houseplace. Some of the houses are still roofed with the thick
and heavy local 'flags', some have the original stone lintels over
their front door, inscribed with the initials of the owner and the
date of building. The latter offers evidence that the average older
building was put up around 1700; before this date there were
few stone houses in the area. Dominating the village is the
limestone quarry (giving welcome employment but whose great
buildings all too often give off clouds of black smoke as the
furnaces reduce the rock to lime).

There are two shops in the village, one doubling as post office
and grocer, the other as a café which sells cards, maps and
guidebooks as well as badges, souvenirs and refreshments. It is
called the Penyghent Café and trades successfully and usefully
on the fact that Horton is a staging-post on the Pennine Way,
and on the Three Peaks walk; an added bonus comes from the
crowds who gather for the annual Three Peaks Race, held on the
third Saturday in April, which begins and ends at Horton.

A clocking-in machine, in itself a fine antique, is installed in

the café. Prospective walkers, thinking of attempting all three Peaks in one day, are asked to fill in their clocking-in card with useful details, including home telephone number, car registration number, and where parked. Those who return in less than 12 hours claiming to have done all Three receive a certificate. Those who don't clock-out after twelve hours, and whose car is still where they said they had left it, are then 'investigated'. Only very seldom are rescue teams called out.

But the Cave Rescue Organisation deserves more than a mere mention. In many ways it resembles the RNLI. But it is a local institution, based at Clapham. More than a hundred volunteers are permanently on call, and firms or farmers respect the need to release rescuers at a moment's notice in an emergency. The first responsibility for rescue lies with the Settle police, who call on the CRO when necessary. Funds for equipment – they have two Land Rovers and, of course, ladders and other necessary gear – come largely from donations (especially from those who have been rescued) and there is also a small grant from the Yorkshire

Dales National Park. Most of their rescues, in fact, are 'surface jobs', people who fall and break a leg, who get stuck in a bog, or simply lose their way in the mist (unexpectedly easy to do). The dramatic rescues which get reported on the News are rare, and the reaction of shocked amazement that 'people can be so stupid' is in fact not so often expressed by the rescuers as by the public.

The Three Peaks Race takes place normally at the end of April. The event originated in 1892, when two masters from Giggleswick School timed themselves over the course. Little could they have realised that they were initiating a national event that today attracts hundreds of runners, thousands of spectators, but no money for the winner. To break the record, he or she (for more and more women enter each year) would have to cover the twenty or more miles of marshy, often partially snowcovered steep up-and-down course in less than two hours 26 minutes, for this was the winner's time in 1968. But a normal walker, seeking enjoyment, some acclaim and perhaps sympathy might do the Three in ten hours.

The race has not been popular with farmers. The runners used to map their own route, and often kept it a secret from others; they were not too careful about which fields they crossed. Spectators could be worse, climbing on or over walls to get a good view or a good photograph. And they left gates open. Nor is this the extent of their thoughtlessness. They did not always realise that at the end of April many of the sheep have just given birth; they suffer from post-natal tension too, and they're exhausted. They don't like being disturbed by shouting supporters, whom they easily mistake for farmers bringing them hay, only to have their expectations dashed. Recently a bit of order has been established by the Yorkshire Dales National Park wardens co-operating with the farmers and race organisers. The number of runners has been limited to 200, a single official route has been agreed upon, and spectators are curbed.

At the end of the summer there is a strange repetition of the race, this time on bicycles, or rather with bicycles. The competitors carry their feather-weight machines up the steepest slopes, ride them down, and speed along the roads between the Peaks. But so far they have not beaten the record of the runners.

Of all the old buildings in Horton the one most worth attention is the little church of St Oswald. The squat little tower dates from the fourteenth century, but the chancel and nave, all under one roof, were built earlier. In the chancel the arches are pointed, in the nave they are semi-circular. The south door and font are decorated with a zig-zag Norman pattern. The pillars on the south side have a distinct bias southwards, and so does the south wall of the church. It is said to be safe. The glass does not appear to be interesting, but the plain west window has a little piece of pre-Reformation glass set in it which shows a mitred head, with letters roughly scratched beside it, reading: 'Thomas Cantuar' (it is presumed to be Thomas à Beckett). Another fragment has been identified as part of the coat of arms of Jervaulx Abbey, which was one of three monasteries which owned land in the neighbourhood, the others being Fountains and Furness. Various tales are told in connection with the lead roof. As part of the restoration in 1825, the original lead was stripped, melted down to extract the silver, and replaced. This proved so unsatisfactory that it had to be replaced again 50 years later. The suggestion that the lead came from Hull Pot, a couple of miles away, is unproven and unlikely. Two lych gates seem rather excessive for a small cemetery – presumably this saved the pall-bearers a few steps. (The word 'lych' is connected with the German 'Leich' – corpse – and the lych gate was where the bearers rested the coffin on the edge of the churchyard, to await the arrival of the parson.) The roofs of both gates are made of huge flagstones from the Helwith Bridge Quarry. This quarry works at full pressure today. It is a beautiful example of massive and modern industrial enterprise. In this quiet rural setting the rock is blasted off in great slabs, and crushed and sorted out in the towering buildings embedded in the quarry bottom.

But long ago, when the cutting and crushing machines were operated by a waterwheel in the nearby Ribble, this quarry supplied a number of the headstones in the churchyard, some of which are carved with great care, the writing sometimes surmounted with the flower of an Ox-Eye Daisy which grows plentifully nearby. Two examples of these carvings are to be seen on stones outside the south porch, one on the east side and one on the west.

But to return to the Crown and to walking. From the top of the yard outside the pub Harker Scar Lane, a 'green road', leads along the flank of Penyghent into Langstrothdale. The latter has been tastelessly carpeted with a huge crop of Christmas trees by the Economic Forestry Co., but the walk suggested here breaks off before reaching this unnatural example of rural industrialisation. The first few miles of the road from Horton follow the Pennine Way, which leads on to Hawes and to Northumberland. The road slopes gently upwards, giving side-face views of Ingleborough on the left and Penyghent on the right; one cannot help wondering why the idiosyncratic ends of each, shaped like the lower half of a C, occur at the north end of Ingleborough, and the south end of Penyghent. The best explanation is that each was formed by two separate rivers that once flowed, one from the north past Ingleborough towards the

The Three Peaks Race

sea and the other from the direction of Malham Moor into what became the Ribble valley. Each deposited silt which, by being pressed down by hundreds of feet of sea water over millions of years, became millstone grit.

The early part of Harker Scar Lane is straight and featureless, so this might be the moment to consider the walls on either side and to reflect on the building and composition of dry stone walls. These often appear almost to grow out of the ground they rest on, so natural and almost organic do they seem. On either side of the lane near Horton, they are made of large brown stones, sandstone from the Yoredale Series. They are rounded and smooth, having been trundled along at the bottom of the glacier as it crept down this valley. They were deposited here when the last glacier melted, and provided material for the wall because wall builders never went very far to collect their stones, nor did they have to dig deep to get them.

But higher up the lane white, sharp-angled limestones share a place in the wall alongside the mudstone, and then, after a few yards, the limestone takes over, these stones being taken from the Great Scar Limestone over which the path now runs. However, the take-over is not complete. It is noticeable that the 'throughs', the bigger flat stones which jut out on each side of the wall and give it strength, are of brown Horton slate, quarried from the now-abandoned Arco Wood Quarry south of Horton. But some of the gate-posts in the wall, standing as much as six feet high and having a bluish tinge, will have come from the Helwith Bridge Quarry, where these slabs of Silurian mudstone stand almost vertical, piercing the Great Scar Limestone. Until about 60 years ago these huge 'slates' were extracted and cut for a multitude of uses locally: besides gate-posts, headstones and roofing tiles, these massive smooth flags were used for the sides of outdoor water cisterns (sealed with lead), partitions between cattlestalls (when they were called 'boskins'), for farmhouse floors and for the wide shelves of dairies.

Dry-stone Walls

The dry-stone walls on and around the Three Peaks are of three kinds. Those close to a village will be irregular, and often rather untidily built. These originally enclosed 'crofts', small fields, often rocky, near to houses. They date from the sixteenth century, when 'cottagers were allowed to enclose small crofts of ground immediately surrounding their houses for the growing of special crops, hemp for linen, and grain for their own use or for their animals' (Raistrick: *The Pennine Walls*, Dalesman).

Evidence for this becomes clearer from a study of the leases of houses, which show that an average house had with it four or five closes or crofts, often also giving the right to procure walls round the crofts. These walls are clumsily put together, often winding a bit to include immovable boulders and so save labour. As Raistrick writes: 'such walls are curly and bulging, hardly a straight line to be found among them'.

The Enclosure Acts of the late eighteenth century divided up land that had been common land into 'allotments', often rectangular fields bounded by straight walls; in the valley bottoms, where the land was fertile, these were usually quite small, eight to ten acres.

Then higher up on the slopes come the new 'common' lands which would be sold or let by the Lord of the Manor to 'graziers' as 'gaits' (see page 161). The latter areas, and sometimes parish boundaries, were designated by the miles-long straight walls which climb the upper hillsides, often undeterred even by gradients of one in one.

The Commissioners responsible for enforcing the Enclosure Acts in the eighteenth century often specified in great detail the nature and dimensions of the walls which would surround the enclosure pastures. In 1788 the Commissioners who were concerned with the enclosures around Grassington wrote that:

> The same shall be done by good stone walls in all places made 34 inches broad in the Bottom and 6 Feet high. . . There shall be laid in a Workmanlike manner 21 good Throughs in every Rood . . . the first twelve to be laid on at a height of 2 Feet from the ground, and the Wall at that height to be 2 Feet broad, and the second 9 to be laid on at a height of 4 Feet . . . etc, etc.

Ornamental capping to a dry-stone wall

The advantages of dry-stone walls are many, not the least being that they can stand up to high winds, because they 'filter' them without causing turbulent whirlwinds on the lee side. Yet they provide valuable shelter for sheep against the wild west winds and the driving rain; perhaps more important, during the typical heavy snowfalls drifts build up on the lee side, and these often contain and preserve the sheltering sheep, which 'breathe' hollows for themselves, natural igloos as it were, until dogs with sharp noses, and men with blunt sticks, come and seek them out. These walls don't need the annual attention which hedges do, and their construction uses up the stones from the nearby fields, thus doing a double favour to the farmer.

It is true that they do use up a great quantity of stone; about a ton goes into a yard of six-foot wall. And they take time to build; a good waller expects to do only six yards in a day, even with a mate working 't'other side o' t'wall'. Nor has modern

technology come up with any labour-saving devices: the real waller even spurns rubber gloves; he likes to feel the stone on his fingers! But it is satisfying work; you can't go to sleep on the job, because the whole time you are exercising judgement, and testing your skill in a really worthwhile exercise in 'spatial relationships'.

The most important part of the wall lies a few inches, seldom as much as a foot, below the surface of the turf. Here the 'footings', heavy stones with at least one squared side facing outwards, are firmly laid on each side of the foundation trench. The space between is carefully filled up with small stones. When this bottom course is solid and flat, the wall is properly 'bedded', and should last for ever. The double wall is then begun, one course at a time, each stone resting on two below, and the gap between the two sides kept level with well-chosen 'fillings' – small stones which are not thrown in, but carefully placed so they bind together as the wall grows. The outer stones should never lean inwards (a temptation beginners need to resist). They should be placed flat and horizontal, but each course a few millimetres in from the one below. This is to get the correct 'batter' (i.e. slope), since the top of the wall is generally about half the width of the bottom. When a wall runs along a slope, the batter is concentrated on the downhill side, for obvious reasons. The tops of walls, called the 'capping', vary almost, one might think, with the whim of the builders; generally they consist of flat stones leaning slightly one way and spanning the two sides of the wall, holding them together. This holding or binding is of course the function of the 'throughs', without which a wall of any size will not survive. It is worth looking at the barns planted in the fields; here the 'throughs' jut out conspicuously. However, after a week or so of hard frost, parts of walls tend to tumble down. The ice has widened the space between the stones, slightly dislodging the carefully constructed handiwork, and, come the thaw, the upper part of the wall falls away. Robert Frost was no doubt referring to the process when he wrote: 'Something there is that does not love a wall, that wants it down.'

Holes in the wall, to let sheep through but keep cattle in, are, in this part of Yorkshire, called cripple holes. Presumably the cripples were dragging a leg, and moved along at knee height. In other parts of Britain they may be called lunky holes, smoot holes or sheep smooses. They are best made at the same time as the wall, and paved; long stones placed vertically form the sides to keep the 'filling' from falling out, and a large flat stone is laid across the gap at the top as a lintel. The same rules apply for water holes to let becks through the wall, and here the lintel needs to be above normal flood level if the flood water is not to wash the 'fillings' away after a few years. The wider streams or dried up beds of streams are sometimes spanned by watergates. These are ingenious constructions. They are hung from the top bar, and attached at each end to the boundary walls which come down to a point as near as possible to the edge of the water. When the stream is full, they 'give' from the bottom, pushed out by the current; but where there is little or no water, the gate falls back vertically. This effectively prevents sheep from straying across the boundary when wandering in the river bed. These interesting reminders of the fall of President Nixon are known locally as 'waterfleacks'.

Sometimes one hears that the art of dry-stone walling is disappearing, and certainly many of the walls around the Three Peaks area are being allowed to crumble. This is partly due to the farmers buying up fields immediately adjacent to their original property, for farms have got bigger and bigger in the past twenty years; clearly it isn't worth keeping a wall in repair if it merely divides one of your own fields from another of your own fields. However there are still many occasions when dry-stone walls need to be maintained. The farmer wants to keep stock in one field rather than another in order to let the grass grow or keep the stock separate. Walls on the sides of roads need to be in good order to stop sheep straying from the pasture, for sheep like to lick the salt from road surfaces which have been treated for snow. In areas where the grykes are deep and concealed, as in woods, the fissures act as sheep or calf traps. This means that the surrounding wall is worth preserving. So although post and wire fences have in many cases replaced the walls, fencing is not cheap, and if the gap in the wall is not too wide, it is worth half a day's work in the slacker winter period to fill it in, 'workmanlike', and to replace with well-laid stone the old bedstead or gate that may have been put there as a temporary stop-gap.

So walling still goes on. It is not too difficult to learn how to do it. Many farmers' children soon learn from their dad or his farm hand. Finally the Dales National Park has insisted that the North Yorkshire County Council Highways Department, when they re-route a road, build walls in the traditional manner. They are made by locals and most of them are a model for anyone to copy.

About a mile along the green lane the track suddenly widens for a few yards. This is where people who have tried to go up in cars or a Land Rover have to turn back. The track ahead is rock-bound and hardly suitable for motorists; and the 'turntable' space here is warning enough for them not to proceed. Wheeltracks are evidence that they have heeded the warning. But as the guide said to Walter White in Clapdale, 'It's a wonder to me that people shouldn't know how to behave themselves.' This is, after all, marked as a bridle path, and once, seeing a car turning at the turntable, I recalled an incident when I was walking a similar path not far from Cambridge with a friend of mine, the somewhat eccentric Chief Education Officer, Henry Morris. Suddenly an old Bull Nose Morris Cowley appeared over a rise in the distance driven obviously by a young undergraduate. As the car approached, Henry stood in the middle of the road – risking, as he said afterwards, his life! But the young man stopped; whereupon Henry beat on the bonnet of the car with his walking stick and, emphasising his words with the beat of his stick, said: 'This is a bridle path; when you have learned to ride a horse you can ride it here. But your car is an illegal intruder and so are you!' He stepped aside. I imagine the driver remembers the incident just as well as I do, but I doubt if I could ever be as outspoken and so effectively irritated. On the occasion when I did see a car in this lane I persuaded myself it must be a farmer with the right to drive here.

After the turntable and another quarter of a mile, the path dips and rises again at Sell Gill. The stream on the right of the track flows reddy-brown and has dyed the rocks over which it runs an attractive russet brown. Just before passing under the

track it falls impressively into a deep narrow fissure in the rocks. It disappears along a pear-shaped channel of rock capped by a huge slab of limestone which forms a Godsbridge for the track to pass over; the stream emerges from under the bridge. Here is the entrance to the Sell Gill pot hole which, I am told, after a ladder descent of several yards opens out into an impressive underground cavern.

Immediately after the gill there is a gate across the track. The Pennine Way branches right, leading past Jackdaw Hole, an open cauldron full of trees and flowers and normally dry. But the left-hand route, leading in the direction of Fawber Farm, may seem the more attractive, especially if the Pennine Way is full of eager walkers. At first the farm buildings cannot be seen, only the trees surrounding it, nor is it necessary to follow the

811745   track all the way down to it. A footpath leads along the 1150' contour, passing up through limestone boulders to a gate in the wall.

Beyond the gate the field is peaty and the path leads past a series of shake holes reminiscent of old bomb craters – inverted cones carpeted with reedy grass. They indicate the presence of water flowing underneath; in a thousand years perhaps they may become pot holes giving access to caves. At the far end of

810755   the field, a gate in the corner leads back onto the Pennine Way. It strikes out due north over pleasant-to-walk-on turf for about half a mile. It seems to be leading directly into those forestry plantations of Langstrothdale, and so it does; but there is a

813772   junction ahead, and a signpost comes into view, pointing left and marked Pennine Way. The path here crosses the moor to

804774   the metalled road and Old Ing, a farmhouse. Originally the inhabited part must have been within the long low building which also used to house the animals. However the whole long building is now nothing but a barn. Presumably about a hundred years ago the owners decided they'd had enough of living so close to the cattle, and built what must have seemed to them a more desirable residence across the yard.

For the last half mile the recommended route has been the same as the one in Chapter 5. For the walkers coming off Penyghent joined the Pennine Way a little further back. But now the routes diverge. Those who came down from the mountain branched right, past Calf Holes to Ling Gill (Chapter 5). Those who went along the side may go on down the road towards High Birkwith but, before reaching it, take a path to

the right, signposted to Nether Lodge. Two fields on, the path crosses Browgill Beck by a Godsbridge – another huge natural slab of limestone under which the stream conveniently flows. Browgill Cave and a fine limekiln justify a slight detour up the right-hand side (the left bank) of the beck; the cave has a fine wide mouth and can be safely explored for about 50 yards. But it would require expert guidance and equipment to try and cover the half mile underground up to Calf Holes (see page 168) where the water enters the system.

The track from the Godsbridge leads to Nether Lodge, a collection of old farm buildings and a 'modern' house, built probably about the same time as the people at Old Ing decided to build their addition (it is a very similar building), but Nether Lodge has been further improved with a picture window, an extension and an outside stairway. The present owners have had the good idea of planting a large number of trees around the house; these will transform the place when they grow tall, and also justify the appendage 'lodge', which originally meant a protected dwelling surrounded by trees.

802770

793778

Birds

The next lap might be thought boring. The now metalled road leads from Nether Lodge for nearly half a mile through a swarm of drumlins, those roughly eliptical hillocks made up of boulder clay: that is, a mixture of debris containing a lot of grit and gravel, which was carried along in the glaciers and dumped in these heaps as the glacier melted. The sharper end of a drumlin is called the lee and is at the downstream end; the upstream end is called the stoss. Most of the contents of these drumlins came from the direction of Hawes to the north-east. As can be imagined, drumlin land cannot easily be improved; the boulder clay holds the water and produces little but rank grass and reeds; even sheep feed there without much relish.

Around here, birds of all kinds can be seen. Some no doubt are attracted by the nearby Ribble and some by the trees and crannies of Ling Gill. There may be oyster catchers and red-shank, the former with a very red beak and the latter with very red legs. They are probably only on a visit from the seaside, possibly looking for a nursery. Certainly that is the reason for

Water hole in a dry-stone wall

194

the curlews coming here; they fly in from Morecambe Bay in springtime to make rudimentary nests in the grass, to lay their eggs and train their young. Their call fills the air – a mournful two-note cry or a sharp repeated alarm call. They are huge – two feet long, with six inches of curved and useful beak. They fly gracefully, effortlessly across the moorland. I was shocked to read in Protheroe's *Natural History of the World* that the curlew is 'greatly pursued by sportsmen, partly on account of its wild shy habits and partly because its flesh is very delicate and well flavoured'. And I was greatly relieved to learn that in the Wildlife Bill of 1981 the curlew had become a protected species.

This will be a disappointment, no doubt, to sportsmen. In Volume III of the *Lonsdale Library of Sports, Games and Pastimes* (Seeley Service, London) we read that 'as sporting birds Curlew are hard to beat . . . occasionally there may be a chance of bagging several birds in quick succession as they swoop round a dog (or it may be a dead relative floating in the tideway) – an advantage which may be fairly taken, as later in the season they become almost as un-getattable as wild geese.' The author further suggests that 'they are quite good eating if taken early in the season. . .'

This reminds me of the heron which I once saw not a quarter of a mile from Nether Lodge. One spring morning I was walking up the stream-bed of Ling Gill (recently protected by the Nature Conservancy Council). I had reached the part where huge irregular cliffs rise up on each side, with trees and bushes growing out of cracks and ridges all the way up. I rounded a slight bend, and there standing in the water, fishing, was a heron. I stopped, and at the same moment the heron rose as if it were filled with helium. It seemed to rise into the air and over the trees on the cliff tops without exertion, without fuss, and without a sound. A beautiful performance. And yet the fish warden who works for the trout hatchery belonging to the Manchester Anglers Club down the valley is said to have told some farmers that he'd be pleased to hear of a heron being shot, because they ate so many of his fish.

What strange philosophies these sportsmen develop. I prefer that incomparable naturalist W.H. Hudson, who writes, in *The Book of a Naturalist* (Wildwood House, 1980), about the heron as 'A Feathered Notable'. He describes vividly the ways of heron and of their young, but also tells a very funny story called 'The Heron as Table Bird'. Two sisters who lived with their rather frightening brother told Hudson how the brother had once brought back a heron he had shot and insisted on their cooking it after it had hung for a few weeks.

> The painful task had to be performed and they loyally went to work and plucked it . . . they finished the hateful business by singeing it and pumping many gallons of water over its carcase . . . and put it in the oven to bake. The smell of it was very trying and . . . pervaded the whole house. The brother, when he sat down, smiled on them approvingly. The heron was brought in, and the brother rose to carve it and heaped their plates with generous slices of the lean black flesh. . . They pretended to cut and eat it while confining themselves to the vegetables on their plates. Their brother was not affected by such squeamishness and . . . did honour to the heron by taking a tremendous mouthful. The sisters exchanged frightened glances, wondering at his courage – wondering too if he would be able to consume the whole monstrous plateful. Then something happened; a change came over his face, he turned pale and stopped chewing; then, mouth still full, he rose and fled from the room.

This, I feel, is a moral tale directed at those who insist on eating protected birds.

Another common sight hereabouts is the lapwing – known also as the Green Plover, the peewit, and locally as the Tew-wit. Peewit, a local name, is clearly onomatopoeic; lapwing, I had thought must at one time have been flapwing, for when flying they perform acrobatics, flapping forward for a few yards, then turning over and tumbling downwards, picking up speed and rising to right or left. However, the *OED* corrected me. It comes from *Hléapewince*: *hleapen* = to leap, and *winc* = to waiver. The peewit has an easily noticeable crest on the top of its head, but if you don't see this, it may still be a peewit, because it can raise or lower it at will. The nest is a mere scratch in the ground lined with grass. The eggs are well camouflaged – olive-coloured with black/brown spots: a wise arrangement, for there are still restaurants which serve plovers' eggs. The good camouflage is not the only protection against the enemies of their children. The mother-bird has that ingenious habit, if disturbed while sitting on the eggs, of running off, flapping and falling around as if she had broken a wing, in the hope that the vandal will chase her and so miss the eggs.

Kestrels are quite often seen hovering over the hillsides, looking with their telescopic eyes for voles and even for little birds nesting. In spring the swallows return to nest in barns, and throughout the summer the larks start up and hover noisily and musically over the grazing sheep. Robins, blackbirds, chaffinches and tits keep the providers of coconuts and bread-crumbs busy through the winter, but the wrens tend to despise what is put out for them. They probably find enough insects for their tiny bodies in the mossy holes in the dry-stone walls which they visit ceaselessly.

On the open moor, the Meadow Pipit is not uncommon. They tend to run and fly and then run and fly again as a human approaches. Finally, another summer visitor, arriving in March and leaving in August, is the wheatear. They find limestone mountainsides good places to disport themselves; they must be one of the few birds that have been re-named to please Mrs Grundy. Their country name is Whitearse, for reasons which are obvious to anyone who comes on them from behind.

So much for some of the birds. The road through the
785780
drumlins from Nether Lodge eventually meets the infant Ribble
(which is already about twenty feet across) and goes over it by a
rather uncertain bridge made from old railway sleepers laid on
780780
an iron frame. Directly ahead Lodge Hall, a fine upstanding
house, has by now come into view; it used to be called Ingman
Lodge, and it stands on the valley side, looking out over the
drumlins to Penyghent, one of the finest buildings, if not the
finest, in the whole area. In spite of the date on the lintel it has
almost an Elizabethan air about it. Unlike most of the houses
hereabouts which wisely face south, Lodge Hall faces east. The
windows are glazed with diamond-shaped panes set in lead. In
the south-east corner is a strange little window set in the angle
of the wall and facing both southwards and eastwards. The front
door is impressive, with a heavy carved stone arch above it and
a date-stone set under the arch and carved **C W 1687**. On each of
the stone uprights either side of the door a halberd is carved.
There is a suggestion that this was a not uncommon habit in the
seventeenth century, when aspiring gentry who would have
liked to have armed footmen guarding their doors settled for
these cheaper substitutes. The same feature can be seen at New
Hall at Rathmel near Settle.

The front entrance leads through an internal porch to the
living room, and in the opposite wall a passage leads through to
the main staircase, which is built of stone slabs, with great stone
slates forming the half landings. The stairs lead up to the first
and second floors. On the first floor are three bedrooms, the
front room at the south end having a little powder closet in the
corner, lit by the small oval window which is visible from
outside at the front. A powder closet has no connection with
today's coyly euphemistic powder room. It was the little room
where the ladies and the gentlemen in the eighteenth century
went to have their wigs powdered; the scented flour must have
flown all over the room. In *The Gamester* (1705) a Mrs
Cunnington described the powdering of wigs:

> The gentleman, wearing a powdering jacket . . . sat in a
> chair, protecting his face and eyes with a paper mask or a
> funnel-shaped nose-bag; the barber, using a bellows or large
> powder puff, enveloped his client's head in powder which
> adhered to the pomatum already applied.

The second floor, where the roof beams are in a sad state of disrepair, contains the attics, and no doubt it was here that the servants slept.

The initials on the door stand for Christopher Weatherhead, a Quaker who bought the house and evidently re-built it in the year marked on the date-stone. People have been living on the site for centuries. Like Nether Lodge and Colt Park, it was a grange of Furness Abbey. It is said to have served as the judge's lodgings for the Assize circuit, and this gave it the older name of 'Angman's (Ingman's) Lodge. Another legend has it that murder was committed in the upstairs bedroom next to the powder closet, where a stain on the boards (today concealed under the lino) remains as evidence.

There is a Quaker burial ground under the trees opposite the house, and nearby the ruined walls of a building that may have been a Meeting House. On the same side of the track is a circular stone construction about ten feet high. It was built between the Wars to serve as a silo, but it is no longer in use. Opposite the former silo is a great stone trough into which water flows continuously from a pipe; usually a cup stands beside the pipe and a notice reads: 'Drinking Water – Free'. A friendly message for walkers doing the Peaks.

777782 The track leads on up to the Horton-Ribblehead road, joining it only a third of a mile from Ribblehead, passing the row of 774785 Railway Cottages on the left. These stand at right angles to the road and look, even after 100 years, somewhat out of place in this rural scene. The Midland Railway used the same design for their cottages, which were built solidly to house their employees, all along the line; the architects' plan were followed whatever the setting. At the bottom of a dip lies Gauber, a small farm whose barn, a little further along the road, has a roof which dips like a horse's back. Beyond lies a meadow with a 773792 name (on the map) which calls out for explanation. The name is Dismal. It gives credibility to the 'Angman Lodge story. Surely the meadow once bordered the crossroads where the old road from Horton met the turnpike road leading from Lancaster to Richmond.

Those who know their *Shropshire Lad* and who pass that way on a cold moonlight night will surely recall:

On moonlit heath and lonesome bank
The sheep beside me graze;
And yon the gallows used to clank
Fast by the four cross ways.

A careless shepherd once would keep
His flocks by moonlight there,
And high amongst the glimmering sheep
The dead man stood on air.

Housman added a footnote which read: 'Hanging in chains was called keeping sheep by moonlight.'

But what a gloomy note on which to end a walk. Best make quickly for the Station Inn, and perhaps stay with *The Shropshire Lad* and Housman, who in the penultimate poem asked:

Say, for what were hop-yards meant
Or why was Burton built on Trent? . .

And as one enters this or any pub, it's worth recalling his next observation (not bad for a professor of Latin):

And malt does more than Milton can
To justify God's Ways to man.

Coda

When Gibbon penned the last words of his *Decline and Fall of the Roman Empire* it was, it is said, 'with a sober melancholy that he parted from his labours'. I shall not compare this little guide to *Decline and Fall*, and I must admit that I felt some relief at getting to the end of these six exhausting walks, comforted by the thought that I could still do other walks over and around the Three Peaks in the future.

Yet I was also sorry to reach the er d, and I continually recall little gems I would have liked to include. But there is a bright side to this, for it means that readers will be able to provide their own addenda, and possibly their own errata. I apologise for the latter but not for the former; there are always gaps to be filled, titbits of history, geology, facts about the fauna and flora to be picked up by the curious visitor.

The area, 'my area' as I have come to call it, does have a peculiar delight. Nothing can rob it of that; nothing can prevent me or other visitors in the future from enjoying and sharing this special delight. As for the backwards looks I have taken as I went over the landscape, I hope they will have fulfilled my aim of sharing the past as well as the present and future. As Herbert Read wrote about 'his area' in 'Moon's Farm':

> Once it was different
> That was in the time of the holy men
> monks who came over the moor
> from the abbey by the sea. . .
> Their path
> led up the dale and across the hills
> and on the hills they had many sheep
> and cattle in the meadows below the hills.

They dammed up the becks
to make fishponds
and ran off a sluice
to drive the millwheel. . .
And yet
there is still something.
I still feel
the Spirit of the Place. . .
It was made up of so many things:
the shapes of these hills
and the changing shadows
the cries of the birds
and the lapping of the stream over the pebbles.
But more than that –
a sense of glory and yes
a sense of grief.
Glory in the present moment
Grief because it was all so momentary
so fleeting. . .

Institutions and Organisations

Yorkshire Dales National Park

National Park Centre: Clapham Tel: Clapham (046 85) 419
Open from April till October.

Administrative Centre: Yorebridge House, Bainbridge,
Leyburn, North Yorkshire. Tel: Wensleydale (0969) 50456

The Centres provide information on many aspects of the
National Park in the form of leaflets and other publications. A
tape/slide show and library are available at Clapham.

The Field Service of the National Park is responsible for
seeing that bridleways and footpaths are maintained, for the
tidiness of the area, and for signposting routes.

The YDNP Committee is the planning authority and tries to
fulfil its obligations 'to maintain and enhance the natural beauty
of the area', by seeing that campsites, new buildings etc., do not
spoil it.

The Committee provides a service for visitors and residents
through the Dales Rail Project on the Settle-Carlisle Railway.
Full details of these special trains are available from the National
Park Centres. For passengers on the Dales Rail trains a selection
of optional guided walks are organised. Guided walks can also
be undertaken from various centres in the summer season.

Whernside Cave and Fell Centre

Dent, Sedbergh, Cumbria LA10 5RE Tel: Dent (058 75) 213

The Centre is a converted Georgian House 1½ miles east of
Dent, standing in its own grounds with dormitory
accommodation, a separate self-catering unit and a camping
field. It is owned by the National Park. A variety of courses in
caving and fellcraft is available. Groups or individuals are
welcome. Programme and full details from the Warden.

Steam Trains

The Steam Locomotive Operators' Association organise steam-hauled trains on the Settle-Carlisle line. Full details with dates and times can be obtained from S.L.O.A. 44 Stafford Rd, Lichfield, Staffs, WS13 7BZ.

During the summer B.R. also operate steam trains along the route. Details from B.R.

Youth Hostels

Dent About three miles from the village along the Hawes Road (SD 774851)

Ingleton In the middle of the village near the swimming pool (SD 696734)

Nature Conservancy Council

Archbold House, Archbold Terrace, Newcastle NE2 1EG Tel: (0632) 816316

Three Nature Reserves in the area are protected by the NCC: Colt Park Wood, Scar Close should be entered after obtaining a permit from Newcastle. Ling Gill has 'open access', but as explained in the text this can be hazardous.

Yorkshire Naturalists Trust

20 Castlegate, York. Tel: (0904) 59570

Responsible for protecting the quarry at Salt Lake and the South House pavements. Permits can be obtained from the above address.

Museums

Museum of North Craven Life Victoria Street, Settle
As its name implies this is a Folk Museum, run by the North Craven Heritage Trust.

Pig Yard Museum Settle
This small museum contains a number of fascinating local finds, particularly from the Victoria Cave at Settle.

Further Reading

The Hon John Byng 5th Viscount Torrington (1743-1813)
The Torrington Diaries Edited by Bruyn Andrews (1934-38)
Pub. Eyre and Spottiswood.
John Byng, nephew of the famous admiral executed '*pour encourager les autres*', made long tours on horseback through the whole of England, writing his diary each evening.

John Housman
'A Descriptive Tour and Guide to the Lakes, Caves, Mountains and other natural curiosities in Cumberland, Westmoreland and Parts of the West Riding of Yorkshire.' Printed by F. Jolloe and sold by C. Law, Ave Maria Lane, London (1802)

The Rev. John Hutton (1740-1806)
'A tour to the Caves in the Environs of Ingleborough and Settle in the West Riding of Yorkshire, with some philosophical conjectures on the Deluge, remarks on the origins of fountains and observations on the ascent and descent of vapours'
Printed for Richardson and Urquhart under the Royal Exchange. J. Robson, New Bond Street and W. Pennington, Kendal (1781)
John Hutton was Vicar of Burton in Kendal. He was the first to write in any detail about the caves and potholes of the area. The book is written in the form of a letter to Thomas Pearson Esq., of Burton in Kendal.

Walter White (1811-1893) *A Month in Yorkshire* Pub. Chapman and Hall (1858)
White was the son of a cabinet maker in Reading. He followed his father's trade for a short time, emigrated to the U.S.A., returned after five years to write: A working man's recollection of America. He became Assistant at the Royal

Society and in 1861 became Librarian. He started making walking holidays abroad, and writing about these, publishing some under such titles as: 'A July holiday in Saxony, Bohemia and Silesia' and 'Mont Blanc and Back.'

William Dobson (1820-1884) *Rambles by the Ribble* Pub. Preston Chronicle (1864)

Dobson was a journalist and antiquary; he became Editor of the Preston Chronicle

J.S. Fletcher *A Picturesque History of Yorkshire* (Three Vols) Pub. JM Dent (1899)

'Being an Account of the History, Topography and Antiquities Of the Cities, Towns and Villages of the County of York, founded on personal observations made during many journeys through the Three Ridings.'

Frederick Riley *The Ribble from its source to the Sea* John Heywood, Manchester (1914)

Kendall and Wroot *Geology of Yorkshire* EP Publishing Co (1924)

Balderson *Ingleton Past and Present* Simpkin and Marshall (1871)

Jacquetta Hawkes *A guide to the Prehistoric and Roman Monuments of England and Wales*. Chatto and Windus (1954)

Arthur Raistrick *The Pennine Dales* Eyre and Spottiswood (1968)

'Pennine Walls' Dalesman (1966)
'The story of Dent Marble' Dalesman (1952)
'The story of the Limekiln' Dalesman (1960)

A. Wainwright *Walks in Limestone Country*, Westmoreland Gazette (1971)

David Crutchley *The Geology of the Three Peaks* Dalesman (1981)

Trevor D. Ford *Ingleborough Cavern and Gaping Gill* (1979)

Coleman *The Railway Navvies* Hutchinson (1965)

Derek Brumhead *Geology Explained in the Yorkshire Dales and Yorkshire Coast*. David and Charles (1979)

Colin Platt *The Monastic Grange in Medieval England* Simpkin Marshall (1969)

J.E. Lousley *Wild Flowers of Chalk and Limestone* Collins (1950)

Geoffrey Grigson *The Englishman's Flora* (Paladin 1956)

Index

Lodge Hall 198
Long Lane 101, 106
Lousley, J.E. 116
lynchets 156

Midland Railway 26, 27, 41, 118, 171, 200

Nature Conservancy Council 139, 169, 195
National Nature Reserve 115, 139
Nether Lodge 193, 194, 195, 198
Newby 126, 127, 129, 130, 131
Newby Cote 126, 127, 130, 131, 136
Nicholson, Norman 23
Norber 103-5

pavements (limestone) 37, 40
Pecca Falls 23
Pennine Way 154, 168, 180, 192
Phillips, John 25, 54
Platt, Robin 128

Raistrick, Arthur 25, 30, 56, 64, 110, 111, 128, 186
Ram Pump, 91
Read, Herbert 201
Ribblehead Viaduct 44, 47, 69, 74
Riley, Frederick 152
Ruskin, John 100

Salt Lake 47, 70, 73, 118, 200
Scar Close 137, 139, 140, 144
Sedgewick, Adam 60, 61
Selside 71, 107, 109, 113, 114, 127
Southey (Robert) 41
Sportsman's Inn 55
Station Inn 10, 54, 144, 171, 172
Storrs Common 125
Studfold 111, 156

Thorns Gill 172
Thornton Force 29, 32
Three Peaks Race 166, 180, 182
Thwaite Lane 103
Torrington, Lord 19, 170
Trow Gill 85, 93, 106, 108

tufa 29, 94
Turbary 37, 38
Turner, J.M.W. 42
Twisleton Lane 31
Twiss 21, 26, 27, 31

Viking Settlement 144

Wainwright, A. 32, 132, 172
Weathercote 42
Whernside Manor 63, 138
Whernside Tarns 66
White, Walter 42, 43, 90, 94, 97, 101, 190
Whitescar Cave 31, 93, 125
Winterscales 44
Wordsworth, William 83

Yordas Cave 32
Yoredale Series 25, 64, 110, 154, 185
Yorkshire Dales National Park 63, 83, 100, 166, 182
Yorkshire Naturalists Trust 70, 118